NPCA National Park Guide

NATIONAL PARKS
AND CONSERVATION ASSOCIATION

GUIDE TO NATIONAL PARKS
SOUTHWEST REGION

Written and compiled by Russell D. Butcher for the National Parks and
Conservation Association and edited by Lynn P. Whitaker

NPCA is America's only private, nonprofit citizen organization dedicated solely
to protecting, preserving, and enhancing the U.S. National Park System. The
association's mission is to protect and enhance America's National Park System
for present and future generations.

Guilford, Connecticut

Photo credits: pages i, 39, 81 © Larry Ulrich; pages iii, vi-vii, 28, 34–35, 37, 42–43, 45,
56–57, 71, 77 © Laurence Parent; pages 1, 15, 76 © David Muench; pages 4, 31 © Carr
Clifton; pages 8, 24–25, 59, 61 © Willard Clay; pages 11, 30, 51, 64–65, 67, 70 © Fred
Hirschmann; page 20 © Jeff Foott; pages 48–49 © Scott T. Smith; page 53 © Tom Till

Maps: © Trails Illustrated, a division of National Geographic Maps
Cover and text design: Adam Schwartzman
Cover photo: Colorado River and Granite Narrows, Grand Canyon National Park, Arizona
(© Larry Ulrich)

Library of Congress Cataloging-in-Publication Data is available

ISBN 0-7627-0577-9

National Parks
and Conservation Association

Thomas C. Kiernan
President

Dear Reader:

Welcome to the National Parks and Conservation Association's national park guidebooks—a series designed to help you to discover America's most significant scenery, history, and culture found in the more than 370 areas that make up the U.S. National Park System.

The park system represents the best America has to offer for our natural, historical, and cultural heritage—a collection of resources that we have promised to preserve "unimpaired" for future generations. We hope that, in addition to giving you practical information to help you plan your visits to national park areas, these guides also will help you be a more aware, more responsible visitor to our parks. The cautions offered at the beginning of these guides are not to frighten you away but to remind you that we all have a role in protecting the parks. For it is only if each and every one of us takes responsibility that these special places will be preserved and available for future generations to enjoy.

For more than three-quarters of a century, the National Parks and Conservation Association has been America's leading citizen advocacy group working solely to protect the national parks. Whether fighting to preserve the wilderness character of Cumberland Island National Seashore, preventing the expansion of a major airport outside the Everglades, stopping a coal mine at Cumberland Gap, or defeating legislation that could lead to the closure of many national parks, NPCA has made the voices of its members and supporters heard in efforts to protect the resources of our national parks from harm.

We hope that you will join in our commitment. Remember: when you visit the parks, take only pictures, and leave only footprints.

1776 Massachusetts Avenue, N.W., Washington, D.C. 20036-1904
Telephone (202) 223-NPCA(6722) • Fax (202) 659-0650

PRINTED ON RECYCLED PAPER

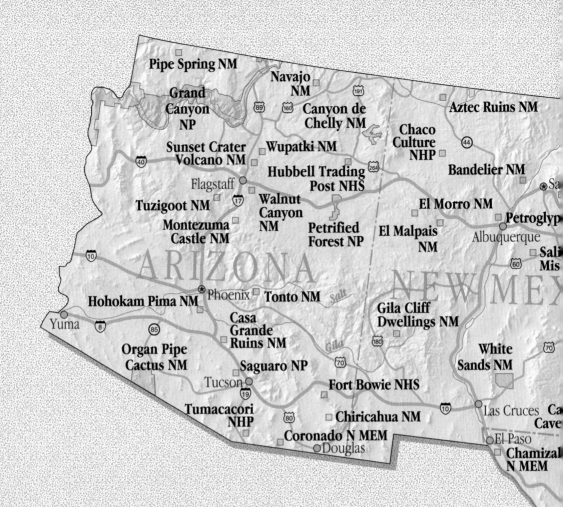

Pipe Spring NM

Navajo NM

Grand Canyon NP

Aztec Ruins NM

Canyon de Chelly NM

Chaco Culture NHP

Sunset Crater Volcano NM

Wupatki NM

Bandelier NM

Flagstaff

Hubbell Trading Post NHS

Tuzigoot NM

Walnut Canyon NM

El Morro NM

Montezuma Castle NM

Petrified Forest NP

El Malpais NM

Petroglyp

Albuquerque

ARIZONA

NEW MEX

Sali Mis

Hohokam Pima NM

Phoenix

Tonto NM

Salt

Gila Cliff Dwellings NM

Yuma

Casa Grande Ruins NM

Gila

White Sands NM

Organ Pipe Cactus NM

Saguaro NP

Tucson

Fort Bowie NHS

Tumacacori NHP

Chiricahua NM

Las Cruces

Ca Cave

El Paso

Coronado N MEM

Douglas

Chamizal N MEM

Southwest Region

ABBREVIATION:

NHP	National Historic
NHS	National Historic
N MEM	National Memor
NM	National Monur
NP	National Park
NRA	National Recreat
NS	National Seasho

NM

Lake Meredith
NRA

Washita Battlefield
NHS

Tulsa

Oklahoma City

Oklahoma City
N MEM

Alibates
Flint
Quarries
NM

Amarillo

ovis

OKLAHOMA

Chickasaw NRA

Lubbock

Lake
Texoma

Fort Worth

Dallas

TEXAS

Pecos

Fort Stockton

Lyndon B.
Johnson
NHP

Austin

Big Thicket
N PRES

io Grande WSR

Houston

Amistad
NRA

San Antonio

San Antonio
Missions NHP

Rio Grande

Corpus Christy

Gulf
of
Mexico

Padre
Island
NS

Palo Alto
Battlefield
NHS

©1989 Trails Illustrated, a division of National Geographic Maps

NATIONAL GEOGRAPHIC MAPS
TRAILS ILLUSTRATED

CONTENTS

▲ *Pueblo Bonito, Chaco Culture National Historical Park, New Mexico*

GENERAL INFORMATION

Whether you're an American history buff or a birdwatcher, a lover of rocky coastlines or marshy swamps, a dedicated environmentalist or a weekend rambler, and whether you're seeking a way to spend a carefully planned month-long vacation or an unexpectedly free sunny afternoon—the national parks are for you. They offer a broad spectrum of natural and cultural resources in all 50 states as well as Guam, Puerto Rico, the Virgin Islands, and American Samoa where you can learn, exercise, participate in activities, and be constantly moved and inspired by the riches available. Perhaps most important of all, as one of the National Park System's 280 million annual visitors, you become part of the attempt to preserve our natural and historical treasures for present and future generations.

This guidebook will help you do that, as one in a series of eight Regional National Park Guides covering all the units in the National Park System. This section of general information provides both an overview of key facts that can be applied to every unit and a brief history of the National Parks and Conservation Association.

SPECIAL PARK PASSES

Some parks charge entrance fees to help offset their operational costs. Several options for special entrance passes are available, enabling you to choose the most appropriate and economical way for you and your family and friends to visit sites.

Park Pass: For this annual entrance permit to a specific fee-charging park, monument, historic site, or recreation area in the National Park System, the cost is usually $10 or $15 depending on the area. Such a pass does not cover any fees other than entrance for permit holder and any accompanying passengers in a private noncommercial vehicle or, in the case of walk-in facilities, the permit holder's spouse, children, and parents. The pass may be pur-

chased in person or by mail from the unit at which it will be used. It is nontransferable and nonrefundable.

Golden Eagle Passport: This annual entrance pass admits visitors to all the federal lands that charge entrance fees; these include national parks, monuments, historic sites, recreation areas, national forests, and national wildlife refuges. The pass costs $50 and is valid for one year from purchase. It does not cover any fees other than entrance for permit holder and any accompanying passengers in a private noncommercial vehicle or, in the case of walk-in facilities, the holder's spouse, children, and parents. The Golden Eagle Passport may be purchased in person or by mail from the National Park Service, Office of Public Inquiries, Room 1013, U.S. Department of the Interior, 18th & C Streets, N.W., Washington, DC 20240 (202-208-4747) or at any of the seven National Park Service field offices, any of the nine U.S. Forest Service regional offices, or any national park unit and other federal areas that charge an entrance fee. It is nontransferable and nonrefundable.

Golden Age Passport: A one-time $10 fee for this pass allows lifetime entrance to all federal fee-charging areas as described in the Golden Eagle Passport section for citizens and permanent residents of the United States who are 62 years of age or older and any accompanying passengers in a private noncommercial vehicle or, in the case of walk-in facilities, the holder's spouse and children. This pass also entitles the holder to a 50 percent discount on use fees charged in park areas. The Golden Age Passport must be obtained IN PERSON at any of the locations listed in the Golden Eagle Passport section; mail requests are not accepted. Applicants must provide proof of age, such as a driver's license or birth certificate, or sign an affidavit attesting to eligibility.

Golden Access Passport: This free lifetime entrance permit to all federal fee-charging areas as described in the Golden Eagle Passport section is available for citizens and permanent residents of the United States who are visually impaired or permanently disabled and any accompanying passengers in a private noncommercial vehicle or, in the case of walk-in facilities, the permit holder's spouse, children, and parents. It also entitles the holder to a 50 percent discount on use fees charged in park areas. The Golden Access Passport must be obtained IN PERSON at any of the locations listed in the Golden Eagle Passport section; mail requests are not accepted. Applicant must provide proof of eligibility to receive federal benefits or sign an affidavit attesting to one's eligibility.

PASSPORT TO YOUR NATIONAL PARKS

The *Passport to Your National Parks* is a special commemorative item designed to serve as a companion for park visitors. This informative and unique publication records each visit through special regional and national stamps and cancellations. When you visit any national park, be sure to have your Passport canceled with a rubber stamp marking the name of the park and the date you were there. The Passport gives you the opportunity to share and relive your journey through America's national parks and will become a travel record to cherish for years. Passports cost $4.95; a full set of ten national and regional stamps are $3.95. The national parks represented in the stamp set vary from year to year. For ordering information, call 800-821-2903, or write to Eastern National Park & Monument Association, 110 Hector Street, Suite 105, Conshohocken, PA 19428.

HELPFUL TRIP-PLANNING PUBLICATIONS

Two volumes offer descriptive text on the National Park System: *Exploring Our National Parks and Monuments,* by Devereux Butcher (ninth edition by Russell D. Butcher), and *Exploring Our National Historic Parks and Sites,* by Russell D. Butcher. These books feature descriptions and black-and-white photographs of more than 370 National Park System units. Both volumes also contain chapters on possible new parks, threats to the parks, a history of NPCA, and the national

park standards. To order, contact Roberts Rinehart Publishers, 6309 Monarch Park Place, Niwot, CO 80503; 800-352-1985 or 303-530-4400.

NPCA offers the following brochures at no charge: *The National Parks: How to Have a Quality Experience and Visiting Battlefields: The Civil War.* These brochures provide helpful information on how best to enjoy a visit to the national parks. NPCA members can also receive the *Park System Map and Guide, The National Parks Index, The National Parks Camping Guide,* and *Lesser Known Areas* as part of NPCA's PARK-PAK by calling 202-223-6722, ext. 214.

The Story Behind the Scenery® and *The Continuing Story®* series are lavishly illustrated books providing informative text and magnificent photographs of the landscapes, flora, and fauna of our national parklands. More than 100 titles on the national parks, historic events, and Indian cultures, as well as an annual national parks calendar, are available. For information, call toll free 800-626-9673, fax to 702-731-9421, or write to KC Publications, 3245 E. Patrick Lane, Suite A, Las Vegas, NV 89120.

The National Parks: Index and *Lesser Known Areas,* both produced by the National Park Service, can be ordered by contacting the Superintendent of Documents, U.S. Government Printing Office, Washington, DC 20402-9325; 202-512-1800. To receive at no charge the *National Park System Map and Guide,* the *National Trails System Map and Guide;* or an *Official Map and Guide* of specific national parks, contact National Park Service, Office of Information, P.O. Box 37127, Washington, DC 20013-7127; 202-208-4747.

National Parks Visitor Facilities and Services is a directory of vendors authorized to serve park visitors through contracts with the National Park Service. Concessionaires offering lodging, food, beverages, outfitting, tours, trail rides, and other activities and services are listed alphabetically. To order, contact the National Park Hospitality Association, 1331 Pennsylvania Ave., N.W., Suite 724, Washington, DC 20004; 202-662-7097.

Great Walks, Inc., publishes six pocket-sized books of detailed information on specific trails

4

◀ *Lower canyons of the Rio Grande, Rio Grande Wild and Scenic River, Texas*

in Yosemite; Sequoia and Kings Canyon in California; Big Bend; Great Smoky Mountains; and Acadia and Mount Desert Island in Maine. For information, send $1 (refundable with your first order) to Great Walks, P.O. Box 410, Goffstown, NH 03045.

The U.S. Bureau of Land Management (BLM) offers free maps that detail recreation areas and scenic and backcountry roads and trails. These are available by contacting the BLM at the Department of the Interior, 1849 C St., N.W., Suite 5600, Washington, DC 20240; 202-452-5125. In addition, *Beyond the National Parks: A Recreational Guide to Public Lands in the West,* published by the Smithsonian Institution Press, is an informative guidebook to many special places administered by the BLM. *America's Secret Recreation Areas,* by Michael Hodgson, is an excellent resource for little-known natural areas in 12 Western states. It details 270 million acres of land administered by BLM, with campgrounds, recreational activities, trails, maps, facilities, and much more. The 1995-96 edition is published by Foghorn Press and is available for $17.95 by calling 1-800-FOGHORN.

The National Wildlife Refuge Visitors Guide can be ordered free from the U.S. Fish and Wildlife Service's Publications Unit at 4401 North Fairfax Dr., MS 130 Webb, Arlington, VA 22203; 703-358-1711.

The four-volume *Birds of the National Parks* by Roland H. Wauer, a retired NPS interpreter and biologist, provides an excellent reference on the parks' birds and their seasons and habitats. This series, written for the average rather than specialist park visitor, is unfortunately out of print.

SAFETY AND REGULATIONS

To protect the national parks' natural and cultural resources and the millions of people who come to enjoy them, the National Park Service asks every visitor to abide by some important regulations. Park staffs do all they can to help

you have a safe and pleasant visit, but your cooperation is essential.

Some park hazards—deep lakes, sheer cliffs, extremely hot or cold temperatures—cannot be eliminated. However, accidents and illnesses can be prevented if you use the same common sense you would at home and become familiar with the park. Take some time before your trip or when you first arrive to get to know the park's regulations, warnings, and potential hazards. If you have children, make sure they understand such precautions, and keep a careful watch over them, especially in potentially dangerous situations. If you are injured or become ill, the staff can help by directing you to the nearest medical center and, in some parks, by giving you emergency care.

A few rules and safety tips are common to many parks. At all parks, you must keep your campsite clean and the park free of litter by disposing of refuse in trash receptacles. The National Park Service also asks you to follow federal regulations and refrain from the abuse of alcohol and the use of drugs, which are often contributing factors to injuries and deaths. Other rules and safety tips are outlined in the "Special Advisories and Visitor Ethics" section; more detailed information may be provided in park brochures, on signs, and on bulletin boards at camping areas and other park sites. The National Park Service asks that you report any violation of park regulations to park authorities. If you have any questions, seek the advice of a ranger.

SPECIAL ADVISORIES AND VISITOR ETHICS

Safe Driving

Park roads are designed for sightseeing, not speeding. Because roads are often narrow and winding and sometimes steep, visitors should drive carefully, observe posted speed limits, and be alert for wildlife, pedestrians, bicyclists, other drivers, fallen rocks or trees, slippery roads, and other hazards. Be especially alert for motorists who might stop unexpectedly for sightseeing or wildlife viewing. Visitors are urged to use roadside pullouts instead of stopping on the roadway.

Campfires

Most parks permit fires, as long as certain rules are followed. To avoid a wildfire that would be dangerous to people, property, and natural resources, parks may allow only certain types of campfires—fires only in grills provided, for example, or in designated fire rings. Firewood gathering may be prohibited or restricted to certain areas, so visitors should plan on bringing their own fuel supply. Fires should be kept under control, should never be left unattended, and should be thoroughly extinguished before departure.

Quiet Hours

Out of respect for other visitors, campers should keep noise to a minimum at all times, especially from 10 p.m. to 6 a.m.

Pets

Pets must always be leashed or otherwise physically restrained for the protection of the animal, other visitors, and wildlife. Pets may be prohibited from certain areas, including public buildings, trails, and the backcountry. A few parks prohibit pets altogether. Dog owners are responsible for keeping their pets quiet in camping areas and elsewhere. Guide dogs are exempted from park restrictions. Some parks provide kennel services; contact the park visitor center for information.

Protection of Valuables

Theft is just as much a problem in the national parks as elsewhere, so when leaving a campsite or heading out on a trail, visitors should take valuables along or hide them out of sight in a locked vehicle, preferably in the trunk.

Heat, Cold, and Other Hazards

Visitors should take precautions to deal with the demands and hazards of a park environment. On hot days, pace yourself, schedule strenuous activities for the morning and evening hours, and drink plenty of water and other fluids. On cold days or if you get cold and wet, frostbite

and the life-threatening illness called hypothermia can occur, so avoid subjecting yourself to these conditions for long periods. In the thinner air of mountains and high plateaus, even those tasks easy to perform at home can leave one short of breath and dizzy; the best advice is to slow down. If a thunderstorm occurs, avoid exposed areas and open bodies of water, where lightning often strikes, and keep out of low-lying areas and stream beds, where flash floods are most likely to occur.

Wild Plants and Animals

It is the responsibility of every visitor to help preserve the native plants and animals protected in the parks: leave them as you find them, undisturbed and safe. Hunting or carrying a loaded weapon is prohibited in all national parks and national monuments. Hunting during the designated season is allowed in parts of only a few National Park System areas, such as national recreation areas, national preserves, and national seashores and lakeshores. While biting insects or toxic plants, such as poison ivy or poison oak, are the most likely danger you will encounter, visitors should be aware of hazards posed by other wild plants and animals. Rattlesnakes, ticks, and animals carrying rabies or other transmittable diseases, for instance, inhabit some parks. Any wild creature—whether it is as large as a bison or moose or as small as a raccoon or prairie dog—is unpredictable and should be viewed from a distance. Remember that feeding any wild animal is absolutely prohibited.

Campers should especially guard against attracting bears to their campsites as a close encounter with a grizzly, brown, or black bear can result in serious injury or death. Park officials in bear country recommend, and often require, that campers take certain precautions. One is to keep a campsite clean. Bears' sensitive noses can easily detect food left on cans, bottles, and utensils or even personal items with food-like odors (toothpaste, deodorant, etc.). Second, food items should be stored in containers provided by the parks or in your vehicle, preferably out of sight in the trunk. Bears, especially those in Yosemite, are adept at breaking into cars and other motor vehicles containing even small amounts of food and can cause extensive damage to motor vehicles as they attempt to reach what they can smell. Third, in the backcountry, food should be hung from poles or wires that are provided or from a tree; visitors should inquire at the park as to the recommended placement. In treeless surroundings, campers should store food at least 50 yards from any campsite. If bears inhabit a park on your itinerary, ask the National Park Service for a bear brochure with helpful tips on avoiding trouble in bear country and inquire if bears are a problem where you plan to hike or camp.

Backcountry Camping

Camping in the remote backcountry of a park requires much more preparation than other camping. Most parks require that you pick up a backcountry permit before your trip so that rangers will know about your plans. They can also advise you of hazards and regulations and give you up-to-date information on road, trail, river, lake, or sea conditions, weather forecasts, special fire regulations, availability of water, and other matters. Backcountry permits are available at visitor centers, headquarters, and ranger stations.

There are some basic rules to follow whenever you camp in the backcountry: stay on the trails; pack out all trash; obey fire regulations; be prepared for sudden and drastic weather changes; carry a topographic map or nautical chart when necessary; and carry plenty of food and water. In parks where water is either unavailable or scarce, you may need to carry as much as one gallon of water per person per day. In other parks, springs, streams, or lakes may be abundant, but always purify water before drinking it. Untreated water can carry contaminants. One of the most common, especially in Western parks, is *giardia*, an organism that causes an unpleasant intestinal illness. Water may have to be boiled or purified with tablets; check with the park staff for the most effective treatment.

Sanitation

Visitors should bury human waste six to eight inches below ground and a minimum of 100 feet from a watercourse. Waste water should be disposed of at least 100 feet from a watercourse or campsite. Do not wash yourself, your clothing, or your dishes in any watercourse.

CAMPING RESERVATIONS

Most campsites are available on a first-come, first-served basis, but many sites can be reserved through the National Park Reservation Service. For reservations at Acadia, Assateague Island, Cape Hatteras, Channel Islands, Chickasaw, Death Valley, Everglades, Glacier, Grand Canyon, Great Smoky Mountains, Greenbelt, Gulf Islands, Joshua Tree, Katmai, Mount Rainier, Rocky Mountain, Sequoia-Kings Canyon, Sleeping Bear Dunes, Shenandoah, Whiskeytown, and Zion, call 800-365-CAMP. For reservations for Yosemite National Park, call 800-436-PARK. Reservations can also be made at any of these parks in person. Currently, reservations can be made as much as eight weeks in advance or up to the day before the start of a camping stay. Please have credit card and detailed camping information available when you call in order to facilitate the reservation process.

BIOSPHERE RESERVES AND WORLD HERITAGE SITES

A number of the national park units have received international recognition by the United Nations Educational, Scientific and Cultural Organization for their superlative natural and/or cultural values. Biosphere Reserves are representative examples of diverse natural landscapes, with both a fully protected natural core or park unit and surrounding land being managed to meet human needs. World Heritage Sites include natural and cultural sites with "universal" values that illustrate significant geological processes, may be crucial to the survival of threatened plants and animals, or demonstrate outstanding human achievement.

▲ *Organ Pipe Cactus National Monument, Arizona*

CHECKLIST FOR HIKING AND CAMPING

Clothing

- Rain gear (jacket and pants)
- Windbreaker
- Parka
- Thermal underwear
- T-shirt
- Long pants and shorts
- Extra wool shirt and/or sweater
- Hat with brim
- Hiking boots
- Camp shoes/sneakers
- Wool mittens
- Lightweight shoes

Equipment

- First-aid kit
- Pocket knife
- Sunglasses
- Sunscreen
- Topographic map
- Compass
- Flashlight, fresh batteries, spare bulb
- Extra food and water (even for short hikes)
- Waterproof matches
- Fire starter
- Candles
- Toilet paper
- Digging tool for toilet needs
- Day backpack
- Sleeping bag
- Sleeping pad or air mattress
- Tarp/ground sheet
- Sturdy tent, preferably free-standing
- Insect repellent
- Lip balm
- Pump-type water filter/water purification tablets
- Water containers
- Plastic trash bags
- Biodegradable soap
- Small towel
- Toothbrush
- Lightweight backpack stove/extra fuel
- Cooking pot(s)
- Eating utensils
- Can opener
- Electrolyte replacement for plain water (e.g., Gatorade)
- Camera, film, lenses, filters
- Binoculars
- Sewing kit
- Lantern
- Nylon cord (50 feet)
- Whistle
- Signal mirror

▲ Mission San José, San Antonio Missions National Historical Park, Texas

A Brief History of the National Parks and Conservation Association

In 1916, when Congress established the National Park Service to administer the then nearly 40 national parks and monuments, the agency's first director, Stephen Tyng Mather, quickly saw the need for a private organization, independent of the federal government, to be the citizens' advocate for the parks.

Consequently, on May 19, 1919, the National Parks Association—later renamed the National Parks and Conservation Association (NPCA)—was founded in Washington, D.C. The National Park Service's former public relations director, Robert Sterling Yard, was named to lead the new organization—a position he held for a quarter century.

The association's chief objectives were then and continue to be the following: to vigorously oppose threats to the integrity of the parks; to advocate worthy and consistent standards of *national* significance for the addition of new units to the National Park System; and, through a variety of educational means, to promote the public understanding and appreciation of the parks. From the beginning, threats to the parks have been a major focus of the organization. One of the biggest conservation battles of NPCA's earliest years erupted in 1920, when Montana irrigation interests advocated building a dam and raising the level of Yellowstone Lake in Yellowstone National Park. Fortunately, this threat to the world's first national park was ultimately defeated—the first landmark victory of the fledgling citizens' advocacy group on behalf of the national parks.

At about the same time, a controversy developed over the authority given to the Water Power Commission (later renamed the Federal Power Commission) to authorize the construction of hydropower projects in national parks. The commission had already approved the flooding of Hetch Hetchy Valley in Yosemite National Park. In the ensuing political struggle, NPCA pushed for an amendment to the water

power law that would prohibit such projects in all national parks. A compromise produced only a partial victory: the ban applied to the parks then in existence, but not to parks yet to be established. As a result, each new park's enabling legislation would have to expressly stipulate that the park was exempt from the commission's authority to develop hydropower projects. Yet this success, even if partial, was significant.

Also in the 1920s, NPCA successfully urged establishment of new national parks: Shenandoah, Great Smoky Mountains, Carlsbad Caverns, Bryce Canyon, and a park that later became Kings Canyon, as well as an expanded Sequoia. The association also pushed to expand Yellowstone, Grand Canyon, and Rocky Mountain national parks, pointing out that "the boundaries of the older parks were often established arbitrarily, following ruler lines drawn in far-away offices." The association continues to advocate such topographically and ecologically oriented boundary improvements for many parks.

In 1930, the establishment of Colonial National Historical Park and the George Washington Birthplace National Monument signaled a broadening of the National Park System to places of primarily historical rather than environmental importance. A number of other historical areas, such as Civil War battlefields, were soon transferred from U.S. military jurisdiction to the National Park Service, and NPCA accurately predicted that this new category of parks "will rapidly surpass, in the number of units, its world-celebrated scenic" parks. Today, there are roughly 200 historical parks out of the total of 378 units. NPCA also pushed to add other units, including Everglades National Park, which was finally established in 1947.

A new category of National Park System units was initiated with the establishment of Cape Hatteras National Seashore in North Carolina. However, in spite of NPCA opposition, Congress permitted public hunting in the seashore—a precedent that subsequently opened the way to allow this consumptive resource use in other national seashores, national lakeshores, national rivers, and national preserves. With the exception of traditional, subsistence hunting in Alaska national preserves, NPCA continues to oppose hunting in all national parks and monuments.

In contrast to its loss at Cape Hatteras, NPCA achieved a victory regarding Kings Canyon National Park as a result of patience and tenacity. When the park was established in 1940, two valleys—Tehipite and Cedar Grove—were left out of the park as a concession to hydroelectric power and irrigation interests. A few years later, however, as the result of concerted efforts by the association and other environmental groups, these magnificently scenic valleys were added to the park.

In 1942, the association took a major step in its public education mission when it began publishing *National Parks*. This award-winning, full-color magazine contains news, editorials, and feature articles that help to inform members about the parks, threats facing them, and opportunities for worthy new parks and offers readers a chance to participate in the protection and enhancement of the National Park System.

In one of the most heavily publicized park-protection battles of the 1950s, NPCA and other groups succeeded in blocking construction of two hydroelectric power dams that would have inundated the spectacularly scenic river canyons in Dinosaur National Monument. In the 1960s, an even bigger battle erupted over U.S. Bureau of Reclamation plans to build two dams in the Grand Canyon. But with the cooperative efforts of a number of leading environmental organizations and tremendous help from the news media, these schemes were defeated, and Grand Canyon National Park was expanded.

In 1980, the National Park System nearly tripled in size with the passage of the Alaska National Interest Lands Conservation Act (ANILCA). One of the great milestones in the history of American land conservation, ANILCA established ten new, and expanded three existing, national park units in Alaska. This carefully crafted compromise also recognized the special circumstances of Alaska and authorized subsistence hunting, fishing, and gathering by rural residents as well as special access provisions on most units. The challenge of ANILCA is to achieve a balance of interests that are often in conflict. Currently, NPCA is working to protect sensitive park areas and wildlife from inappropriate development of

roads and unregulated motorized use, and to ensure that our magnificent national parks in Alaska always offer the sense of wildness, discovery, and adventure that Congress intended.

In 1981, the association sponsored a conference to address serious issues affecting the welfare of the National Park System. The following year, NPCA published a book on this theme called *National Parks in Crisis*. In the 1980s and 1990s, as well, the association sponsored its nationwide "March for Parks" program in conjunction with Earth Day in April. Money raised from the hundreds of marches funds local park projects, including improvement and protection priorities and educational projects in national, state, and local parks.

NPCA's landmark nine-volume document, *National Park System Plan,* was issued in 1988. It contained proposals for new parks and park expansions, assessments of threats to park resources and of research needs, explorations of the importance of interpretation to the visitor's quality of experience, and issues relating to the internal organization of the National Park Service. Two years later, the two-volume *Visitor Impact Management* was released. This document found favor within the National Park Service because of its pragmatic discussions of "carrying capacity" and visitor-impact management methodology and its case studies. In 1993, *Park Waters in Peril* was released, focusing on threats seriously jeopardizing water resources and presenting a dozen case studies.

The association has become increasingly concerned about the effect of noise on the natural quiet in the parks. NPCA has helped formulate restrictions on flightseeing tours over key parts of the Grand Canyon; urged special restrictions on tour flights over Alaska's national parks; supported a ban on tour flights over other national parks such as Yosemite; expressed opposition to plans for construction of major new commercial airports close to Mojave National Preserve and Petroglyph National Monument; opposed the recreational use of snowmobiles in some parks and advocated restrictions on their use in others; and supported regulations prohibiting the use of personal watercraft on lakes in national parks.

Other association activities of the late 20th century have included helping to block development of a major gold mining operation that could have seriously impaired Yellowstone National Park; opposing a coal mine near Zion National Park that would have polluted Zion Canyon's North Fork of the Virgin River; objecting to proposed lead mining that could pollute the Ozark National Scenic Riverways; opposing a major waste dump adjacent to Joshua Tree National Park; and helping to defeat a proposed U.S. Department of Energy nuclear waste dump adjacent to Canyonlands National Park and on lands worthy of addition to the park. NPCA is currently proposing the completion of this national park with the addition of 500,000 acres. This proposal to double the size of the park would extend protection across the entire Canyonlands Basin. NPCA has also continued to work with the Everglades Coalition and others to help formulate meaningful ways of restoring the seriously impaired Everglades ecosystem; is urging protection of New Mexico's geologically and scenically outstanding Valles Caldera, adjacent to Bandelier National Monument; and is pushing for the installation of scrubbers on air-polluting coal-fired power plants in the Midwest and upwind from the Grand Canyon.

The association, in addition, is continuing to seek meaningful solutions to traffic congestion and urbanization on the South Rim of the Grand Canyon and in Yosemite Valley; is opposing construction of a six-lane highway through Petroglyph National Monument that would destroy sacred Native American cultural assets; and is fighting a plan to build a new road through Denali National Park. NPCA has supported re-establishment of such native wildlife as the gray wolf at Yellowstone and desert bighorn sheep at Capitol Reef and other desert parks, as well as urging increased scientific research that will enable the National Park Service to more effectively protect natural ecological processes in the future. The association is also continuing to explore a proposal to combine Organ Pipe Cactus National Monument and Cabreza Prieta National Wildlife Refuge into a Sonoran Desert National Park, possibly in conjunction with Mexico's Pinacate Biosphere Reserve.

In 1994, on the occasion of NPCA's 75th anniversary, the association sponsored a major conference on the theme "Citizens Protecting America's Parks: Joining Forces for the Future." As a result, NPCA became more active in recruiting a more racially and socially diverse group of park protectors. Rallying new constituencies for the parks helped NPCA in 1995 to defeat a bill that would have called for Congress to review national parks for possible closure. NPCA was also instrumental in the passage of legislation to establish the National Underground Railroad Network to Freedom.

In January 1999, NPCA hosted another major conference, this time focusing on the need for the park system, and the Park Service itself, to be relevant, accessible, and open to all Americans. The conference led to the creation of a number of partnership teams between national parks and minority communities. In conjunction with all this program activity, the association experienced its greatest growth in membership, jumping from about 24,000 in 1980 to nearly 400,000 in the late 1990s.

As NPCA and its committed Board of Trustees, staff, and volunteers face the challenges of park protection in the 21st century, the words of the association's past president, Wallace W. Atwood, in 1929 are as timely now as then:

All who join our association have the satisfaction that comes only from unselfish acts; they will help carry forward a consistent and progressive program . . . for the preservation and most appropriate utilization of the unique wonderlands of our country. Join and make this work more effective.

Each of us can help nurture one of the noblest endeavors in the entire history of mankind—the national parks idea that began so many years ago at Yellowstone and has spread and blossomed around the world. Everyone can help make a difference in determining just how well we succeed in protecting the priceless and irreplaceable natural and cultural heritage of the National Park System and passing it along unimpaired for the generations to come.

GRAND CANYON NATIONAL PARK

▲ Mt. Hayden

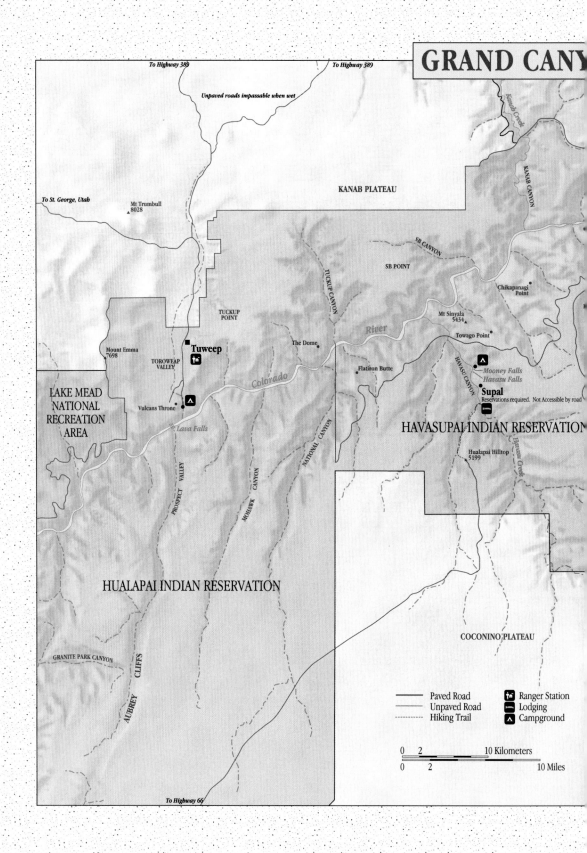

To Highway 389

To Highway 389

Unpaved roads impassable when wet

To St. George, Utah

KANAB PLATEAU

Kanab Creek

KANAB CANYON

Mt Trumbull
8028

SB CANYON

SB POINT

Chikapanagi
Point

TUCKUP CANYON

Mt Sinyala
5434

Towago Point

TUCKUP
POINT

River

Mount Emma
7698

Tuweep

The Dome

Flatiron Butte

HAVASU CANYON

Mooney Falls
Havasu Falls

Supal
Reservations required. Not Accessible by road

TOROWEAP
VALLEY

Colorado

LAKE MEAD
NATIONAL
RECREATION
AREA

Vulcans Throne

Lava Falls

HAVASUPAI INDIAN RESERVATION

Hualapai Hilltop
5199

PROSPECT VALLEY

NATIONAL CANYON

Havasu Creek

MOHAWK CANYON

HUALAPAI INDIAN RESERVATION

COCONINO PLATEAU

GRANITE PARK CANYON

AUBREY CLIFFS

	Paved Road		Ranger Station
	Unpaved Road		Lodging
	Hiking Trail		Campground

| 0 | 2 | | 10 Kilometers |
| 0 | 2 | | 10 Miles |

To Highway 66

Grand Canyon National Park

P.O. Box 129
Grand Canyon, AZ 86023-0129
520-638-7888

Somehow the word "Grand" does not tell how truly incomprehensible the Grand Canyon is. Most people use such adjectives as "magnificent," "stupendous," "incomprehensible," or "awesome"; but mere words of any kind are inadequate to describe this colossal geological creation of nature. The play of light and shadow constantly changes, depending on the angle of the sunlight on the rock strata and formations. When clouds appear, they create contrasting shadows that slide across the vast abyss. The splendor of sunrises, sunsets, and storms takes on an added dimension to match the landscape. The world seems larger here; humans smaller. This is a land to truly humble the soul and inspire the mind.

This 1.2-million-acre national park in northern Arizona protects one of the greatest natural wonders in the world—a canyon that averages ten miles from rim to rim and is more than 15 miles across at its widest; is 277 miles long, where the Colorado River flows through the canyon's Inner Gorge; and is a mile deep from rim to river. Protecting this national treasure has come in stages. Grand Canyon Forest Reserve was established by presidential proclamation in 1893, and Grand Canyon Game Preserve was proclaimed in 1906. Then, Grand Canyon National Monument was proclaimed in 1908, and Grand Canyon National Park was established by Act of Congress in 1919. The park was transferred from the U.S. Forest Service to the National Park Service later in 1919 and was designated a World Heritage Site in 1979. Efforts continue today as NPCA and others support plans to eliminate motor vehicle congestion in the park, to restrict air-tour flights over it and thereby restore natural quiet to major parts of the canyon, and to reduce air pollution that too often impairs the magnificent views.

OUTSTANDING FEATURES

Among the many outstanding viewpoints in the park are the following:

On the South Rim, 25 miles east from Grand Canyon Village, listed from west to east: **Yavapai Point** (7,040 feet elevation), a fabulous canyon view from historic Yavapai Museum, which offers interpretive exhibits and talks; **Mather Point** (7,120 feet), a spot named for the first director of the National Park Service, Stephen T. Mather, and usually the first view of the canyon for visitors entering the park's south entrance; **Yaki Point** (7,260 feet), a grand panorama of the central part of the canyon with South Kaibab trailhead just off the spur road to this point; **Grandview Point** (7,406 feet), a truly grand view with a beautiful woodland of ponderosa and pinyon pines, junipers, and Gambel oaks and the beginning of Grandview Trail; **Moran Point** (7,157 feet), a point named for 19th-century landscape painter Thomas Moran, providing a view of Hance Rapids on the Colorado River and the North Rim's Cape Royal; **Lipan Point** (7,360 feet), a good view of the east end of the canyon and an S-turn of the Colorado River; and **Desert View** (7,438 feet), the highest viewpoint on the South Rim, providing an excellent panorama: to the north, the eastern end of the canyon with a long stretch of the river; to the east, the level expanse of the Marble Platform of the Painted Desert; and 50 miles to the south on the horizon, the ancient 12,643-foot-high volcano known as the San Francisco Peaks.

On the South Rim's West Rim Drive, eight miles west from Grand Canyon Village, listed from east to west are the following: **Trail View Overlook** (6,960 feet), offering a view to the east with Bright Angel Trail below; **Maricopa Point** (7,000 feet), an excellent view of the great geologic fault-line gash of Bright Angel Canyon, extending northeast across Grand Canyon and with the Battleship rock formation below; **Powell Point** (7,040 feet), which features a memorial honoring John Wesley Powell, who led the first river expedition through the canyon in 1869; **Hopi Point** (7,071 feet), a sweeping panorama of a long stretch of the river and an array of tremendous formations rising from the depths of the canyon which is excellent for viewing sunrises and sunsets; **Mohave Point** (6,974 feet), a view northwestward that includes three rapids of the Colorado River; **The Abyss**, the breathtaking east side of which is formed by the 3,000-foot sheer escarpment of the Great Mohave Wall; **Pima Point** (6,720 feet), a good view of the Colorado River and the Tonto Platform, along which winds the Tonto Trail for 70 miles east-west through the canyon; and **Hermit's Rest** (6,640 feet), the westernmost viewpoint, named for Lewis D. Boucher, a French-Canadian who moved to the canyon in the 1890s and took up residence at a spring about a mile west of here.

On the North Rim: **Bright Angel Point** (8,250 feet), a narrow point near Grand Canyon Lodge that offers what is arguably the most awesomely beautiful panorama of the Grand Canyon; **Point Imperial** (8,803 feet), the highest viewpoint on either rim, providing a view of the bold rock formation called Mt. Hayden as well as the beginning of the northeast end of the 12-mile Ken Patrick Trail which, for several miles, offers spectacular views of the northeast end of the canyon from this east edge of the Kaibab Plateau; and **Cape Royal** (7,876 feet), the southernmost viewpoint on the North Rim which includes a spectacular view of the Angel's Window.

PRACTICAL INFORMATION

When to Go

The South Rim is open year-round, while the North Rim, at a thousand feet higher elevation, is normally open from mid-May to mid-October, depending on the weather. The South Rim's West Rim Drive is closed to private motor vehicles from Memorial Day to the end of September, during which time free shuttles are available, departing every fifteen minutes. Another shuttle service operates in the South Rim's Grand Canyon Village. Because parking is often difficult in the summer, visitors are encouraged to park their vehicles in one of the large parking lots and ride the free shuttle.

Hikes into the canyon are best done in spring and fall to avoid extreme temperatures. The prime white-water rafting season on the river is April through October. If you plan a summer visit, the National Park Service advises that you plan well ahead, contact the park, and request a Trip Planner and/or Backcountry Planner to become familiar with park procedures, prices, and schedules. If possible, arrive early in the day and midweek to avoid excessive crowds. For weather and road conditions in the park, call 520-638-7888.

How to Get There

By Car: *To the South Rim's south entrance:* from I-40 just east of Williams, drive north 28 miles on State Route 64 and north 24 miles on U.S. Route 180; or from I-40 at Flagstaff, drive north 75 miles on U.S. Route 180. *To the South Rim's east entrance near Desert View:* from U.S. Route 89 at Cameron, drive west 55 miles on State Route 64. To the North Rim entrance: from U.S. Route Alt. 89 at Jacob Lake, drive south 31 miles on State Route 67, through the Kaibab National Forest. The entire 45-mile scenic route from Jacob Lake south to Bright Angel Point on the North Rim is the state-designated Kaibab Plateau North Rim Parkway. Note: Facilities on the park's North Rim are open from May 15 to October 15, but the road is open later in the year until closed by snow.

By Air: Grand Canyon National Park Airport (520-638-2446) just south of the park in Tusayan is served by scheduled flights from Phoenix, Flagstaff, and Las Vegas.

By Train: Amtrak (800-872-7245) has stops in Flagstaff and operates a bus service to the park. Grand Canyon Railway (800-843-8724) operates a historic steam train between Williams and Grand Canyon Village.

By Bus: Greyhound Lines (800-231-2222) has stops in Flagstaff and Williams.

Nava-Hopi Tours (520-774-5003) operates a bus service from Flagstaff and Williams.

Hourly shuttles run between Grand Canyon Airport, Tusayan, and Grand Canyon Village.

Fees and Permits

Entrance fees are $20 per vehicle and $4 per

person on foot or bicycle. Entrance passes are valid for seven consecutive days, on either or both rims. Permits are required for river running, backcountry camping, fishing, and stock use. Reservations should be made as far in advance as possible for any activity you plan to pursue.

Visitor Centers and Museums

Grand Canyon Visitor Center, at the South Rim's Grand Canyon Village: open daily 8 a.m.-5 p.m. in summer; daily 9 a.m.-5 p.m. in winter. Interpretive exhibits and programs, publications, maps, schedules, and other information.

Yavapai Museum, near Grand Canyon Village: open daily 8 a.m.-6 p.m. in summer; daily 8 a.m.-5 p.m. in winter. Panoramic views from this historic building at Yavapai Point; interpretive programs on canyon geology.

Tusayan Museum and Ruins, near the South Rim's Desert View: open daily year-round 9 a.m.-5 p.m.; closed Christmas and New Year's Day. Cultural/historical exhibits on Anasazi and Hopi Indians, and prehistoric Anasazi pueblo ruin with a self-guided trail.

North Rim Visitor Center, an attractive log building just north of Grand Canyon Lodge: open from May 15 to October 15. Interpretive exhibits, programs, publications, and maps.

Facilities

Numerous gift shops offer such items as hand-made Southwest Indian arts and crafts, publications on the Grand Canyon, and film. At the South Rim's Grand Canyon Village, shops include Hopi House, Verkamp's Curios, and Lookout Studio and gift shops at El Tovar Hotel and Bright Angel, Maswik, and Yavapai lodges. Kolb Studio features books and rotating art exhibits. At the South Rim's Desert View, the Desert View Watchtower provides grand views of the east end of the canyon and beyond and offers Indian arts and crafts in the gift shop. Desert View Trading Post provides a gift shop and snack bar. In summer, Desert View Contact Station is a sales outlet for the nonprofit Grand Canyon Association. On the

North Rim, a gift shop in Grand Canyon Lodge offers such items as publications on the canyon and Indian arts and crafts. On the South Rim, general stores (Babbitt's), open year-round, are located in Grand Canyon Village and at Desert View. On the North Rim, a camper store open from mid-May to mid-October is near the campground about a mile north of Grand Canyon Lodge.

Service stations are located on the South Rim at Grand Village (open year-round) and Desert View (open from April through September); on the North Rim, they are open from mid-May to mid-October near the campground, a mile north of the lodge. For repair services, Grand Canyon Garage is open year-round. For emergencies, call 520-638-2631, ext. 6502.

On the South Rim, the Village Post Office (across the road from the park visitor center) is open Monday through Friday, 9 a.m.-4:30 p.m. and Saturday, 11 a.m.-1 p.m. The postal lobby is open daily from 5 a.m. to 10 p.m. for box access and stamps. Western Union telegraph and fax services are available at the Fred Harvey General Offices, open 8 a.m.-5 p.m. Full-service banking on weekdays is available, including a 24-hour teller machine, cash advances on charge cards, wire services, and foreign currency exchanges.

For worship services on the South Rim, contact the following: Grand Canyon Community Church (inter-denominational), West Rim Worship Site (520-638-2340); Assembly of God, Community Building in Grand Canyon Village (520-638-9415); Grand Canyon Baptist Church, Shrine of the Ages (520-638-9421); Roman Catholic, El Cristo Rey Chapel, Shrine of the Ages (520-638-2390); and Church of the Latter-Day Saints, Shrine of the Ages (520-638-2792). All services are held on Sunday; times vary from year to year.

Handicapped Accessibility

Six accessible sites near wheelchair-accessible restrooms are provided at Desert View campground, and Mather campground also provides accessible restrooms. Many park programs and several paved rim paths are accessible. Contact the park for the Accessibility Guide for detailed descriptions of all facilities.

Medical Services

A medical clinic, the Grand Canyon Health Center (520-638-2551 or 2460) on the South Rim, is open daily. The pharmacy there is open every day but Sunday. A dentist can be reached at 520-638-2395. On the North Rim, first aid is available at Grand Canyon Lodge. The nearest hospitals are in Flagstaff and Kanab, Utah.

Pets

Pets are allowed on leashes on paved rim surface trails, but are prohibited below the rim. Kennel facilities are available at Grand Canyon Village; proof of vaccinations and advance reservations are required (call 520-638-2631, ext. 6039).

Climate

Grand Canyon's climate is characterized by sharply contrasting differences between the rims and deep within the canyon. These contrasts reflect differences in elevation above sea level, ranging from 8,250 feet at the North Rim's Bright Angel Point and 7,120 feet at the South Rim's Mather Point, down to 2,546 feet at Phantom Ranch. Temperatures within the canyon are substantially higher and the air is much drier than on the rims. The average daily temperature range in Fahrenheit and average daily precipitation for higher elevation areas are as follows:

	AVERAGE DAILY	
Month	Temperature F	Precipitation
January	21-42°	1.2 inches
February	26-48°	1.1 inches
March	31-59°	1.3 inches
April	37-69°	0.9 inches
May	49-79°	0.5 inches
June	58-88°	0.5 inches
July	65-94°	1.4 inches
August	63-91°	2.1 inches
September	57-85°	1.0 inches
October	42-68°	0.9 inches
November	31-54°	0.8 inches
December	23-44°	1.4 inches

Safety and Regulations

For your safety and enjoyment and for the protection of the park, please follow these regulations and suggestions:

- Visitors are cautioned to stay on trails, keep safely back from cliff edges and other sheer drop-offs, and watch children closely—especially near the canyon rim.

- Do not hike into the canyon without sufficient water, food, sun protection, and adequate clothing.

- Remember that it is illegal to feed, pet, hunt, capture, or otherwise disturb wildlife in any way. Trees and other plantlife including wildflowers are not to be cut down or picked.

- Be alert for weather changes and beware of thunderstorms and flash flooding.

- Motor vehicles and bicycles must stay on established roads. Hang gliding, rock climbing, fireworks, and all firearms are strictly prohibited in the park.

The National Park Service asks that visitors not litter the park. Remember the excellent slogan to "leave only footprints" as a guide to help protect this national park.

ACTIVITIES

Free ranger-led interpretive activities include nature walks, slide shows, geology and history talks, cultural demonstrations, and children's and campfire programs. Also available in the park are viewing the canyon from scenic overlooks, hiking, photography, picnicking, camping, riding mules into the canyon, bicycling, river rafting and kayaking, fishing, horseback riding, bus tours, and cross-country skiing. Further information is available in the park's newspaper, *The Guide*.

Tours

Harveycar Tours offers experienced guides to escort visitors to major rim viewpoints in comfortable motorcoaches and vans. Call 520-638-2401 or check with the transportation desks in Bright Angel, Maswik, and Yavapai lodges or the concierge desk at El Tovar Hotel for departure times, prices, and reservations.

Among the tour options, Hermit's Rest/West Rim Coach Tour offers two-hour, 16-mile round-trip tours along the West Rim to major viewpoints. On the Desert View/East Rim Coach Tour, experienced guides narrate a 23-mile, one-way tour along the East Rim. A Combination Tour offers both Hermit's Rest/Desert View or Desert View/Sunset Tour at a special price. Sunset Tour is a 90-minute tour through the historic village area at sunset. Monument Valley Expedition offers a 12-hour, 360-mile off-road adventure with a Navajo guide through Monument Valley and a Native American hogan (by special arrangement). The Anasazi Indian Adventure is an 11-hour, 225-mile excursion to explore the various cultures of the region, including a visit to Walnut Canyon National Monument.

Mule Rides

Mule rides into the canyon are available for one day (seven hours round-trip) or two days; call 520-638-2401 for reservations. The overnight trip is especially memorable, with a stay at historic Phantom Ranch near the banks of the Colorado River, a family-style breakfast and dinner, and a hot lunch for the trail. The first day's ride is 5.5 hours; the second day's ride is 4.5 hours. Trips are booked up to a year in advance, so call early. North Rim trips (from mid-May to mid-October) may be easier to book on short notice; check with Grand Canyon Lodge or call 520-638-2292.

Hiking

Hiking at Grand Canyon is easily the best way to get to know the park. It is also potentially the most dangerous activity—especially if you are not properly prepared and neglect precautions given by the National Park Service. Two of the most important precautions are:

1. Take and drink water throughout your hike. You can need as much as a gallon for every day you are hiking.

2. Do not try to hike from rim to river and back to the rim in one day. Unless you are in top physical condition, you are risking disaster by taking such a grueling hike.

Visitors who ignore these and other safety precautions may require emergency evacuation

from the canyon. The several-hundred-dollar cost of the evacuation is borne by the evacuee. Hikers should also wear a hat, use sunscreen, and remember that it usually takes twice as long to hike out of the canyon as it takes to hike in. On trails shared with mules, the mules have the right of way. So when you see a mule train approaching, find a safe place to stand aside and wait quietly until it has passed.

Detailed maps of hiking trails are available at the visitor centers and some of the gift shops. The best place for hiking information and trail conditions is the Backcountry Office, near the entrance of the South Rim's Mather Campground and near the entrance of the North Rim Campground.

Maintained versus Not-Regularly-Maintained Trails

The Rim Trail (South Rim), Bright Angel Trail, North and South Kaibab trails, and several trails along the North Rim including the Transept and Widforss are maintained by the National Park Service. This makes them good choices for relatively inexperienced hikers, since trail finding skills and rock scrambling are not required. The not-regularly-maintained trails, such as the Hermit and Grandview, are generally more remote and steeper and require some form of rock scrambling or even perilous navigation of rock slides.

Hiking Trails

On or from the South Rim: **Rim Trail**, a nine-mile, level trail that follows the South Rim between Mather Point and Hermit's Rest, providing grand panoramas at all major overlooks and other stretches; the trail is paved between Mather Point and Maricopa Point and does not descend into the canyon; **Bright Angel Trail**, a 7.8-mile trail from rim to river with an altitude drop of 4,460 feet, known as the "highway" into the canyon with its trailhead near Bright Angel Lodge; water is available from spring through fall in rest houses 1.5 miles and three miles from the rim and year-round at Indian Gardens at the half-way point and near the Colorado River at the end of the trail; a campground is at Indian Gardens, and lodging and meals are available at Phantom Ranch by reservation; only those who are in

▲ *Krishna Shrine, Vishnu Temple, and Freya*
Castle, Grand Canyon National Park, Arizona

top physical condition should consider hiking
from rim to river and back to the rim in a sin-
gle day, but the round-trip to Indian Gardens
or Plateau Point offers a good, long day hike;
South Kaibab Trail, a 6.3-mile hike from
the rim at Yaki Point to the river with an altitude loss of 4,780 feet and a descent into the
Inner Gorge that is truly spectacular; after the
Bright Angel, South Kaibab is the most popular
trail in the park, but unlike Bright Angel, this
trail begins by following ridge lines that extend
outward into the canyon, thereby offering
spectacular panoramas, and farther down, it is
much steeper in places; hikers are encouraged
not to use this trail to climb out of the canyon,

and hiking it from rim to river and back in one day is strongly discouraged; however, the round-trip to Cedar Ridge makes an excellent and spectacularly scenic day hike; note that water is not available along the trail; **Hermit Trail**, a nine-mile trail that is very rugged and not regularly maintained, proceeding from Hermits Rest on the rim to the river with an altitude drop of 4,250 feet; this steep, rocky trail is for experienced hikers only and requires two tricky scrambles over rock slides that have washed away parts of the trail; water is available at Santa Maria Springs, Hermit Creek, and the river; and **Grandview Trail**, a three-mile trail that is strenuous to climb and not regularly maintained, from Grandview Point to Horseshoe Mesa with an altitude loss of 2,200 feet; this trail is used primarily for backcountry hikers on multi-day, trans-canyon hikes as the trail connects with the trans-canyon Tonto Trail; water is not available along the trail.

On or from the North Rim: **Bright Angel Point Trail**, a paved, quarter-mile path that begins adjacent to Grand Canyon Lodge and provides spectacular views of the canyon; **Transept Trail**, a delightful, 1.5-mile rim trail between North Rim Campground and Grand Canyon Lodge that provides dramatic views of the Transept, the largest tributary canyon of Bright Angel Canyon; the trail leads through beautiful areas of pines, Douglas firs, and aspens, the foliage of the latter turning golden in early October; to return by a different route, hikers may take the bridge path that closely parallels the main road to the lodge; **Uncle Jim Trail**, a pleasant, mostly level, five-mile round-trip forest walk that begins at the North Kaibab Trail parking area, starts at the beginning of the Ken Patrick Trail, and then makes a loop on Uncle Jim Point to a viewpoint overlooking the North Kaibab Trail's switchbacks into the canyon; **Ken Patrick Trail**, a 12-mile, largely level trail that winds through the North Rim forest and along the rim between the parking area for the North Kaibab Trail and Point Imperial, several miles of which run along the east edge of the Kaibab Plateau between Point Imperial and the park road to Cape Royal, providing spectacular views of the northeast corner of Grand Canyon with the Painted Desert stretching eastward; **Widforss Trail**, a five-mile trail starting at a meadow filled with summer wildflowers and offering an essentially level day hike through a North Rim forest of ponderosa pine, Engelmann and blue spruces, Douglas fir, and quaking aspen, ending with a panorama of the canyon at Widforss Point; to reach the trailhead, turn off onto the dirt road that is a quarter-mile south of the junction of the road to Point Imperial/Cape Royal and continue a mile to the Widforss Trail parking area; **Cape Royal Trail**, a level, paved, one-third-mile, self-guided interpretive trail that provides views of the east end of the canyon, the Colorado River, and the spectacular Angel's Window formation; North Kaibab Trail, a 14.2-mile, rim-to-river trail with an altitude loss of 5,816 feet; from the North Rim, the upper part of this route is steep and narrow, but in combination with the South Kaibab or the Bright Angel, this trail is popular for rim-to-rim hikes, with most campers stopping overnight at Cottonwood and Bright Angel campgrounds; lodging and meals at Phantom Ranch are by reservation only; alternatively, a good day hike down the North Kaibab is the 9.4-mile, six-to-eight-hour round-trip hike to Roaring Springs, which are slightly more than 3,000 feet below the North Rim and provide all the drinking water for facilities on both rims of the canyon; mule trips from the North Rim also use the North Kaibab Trail; and **Clear Creek Trail**, a nine-mile hike from the North Kaibab Trail eastward across the Tonto Platform just above the canyon's Inner Gorge to Clear Creek; this fairly well maintained trail provides a good overnight trip from Phantom Ranch or Bright Angel Campground; the hike from the North Kaibab to the Tonto Platform also provides dramatic overlooks of the Phantom Ranch area; water is available at Clear Creek.

Note: All services on the North Rim are closed from mid-October until mid-May.

Rafting

Free permits are required for private river-running trips and can be obtained at the River Subdistrict Office (plan ahead: the waiting list is long). White-water rafting trips of from three days to three weeks are organized by private concessioners. For a complete list, write to the River Permits Office, GCNP, P.O. Box 129, Grand Canyon, AZ 86023. Smooth water trips or 12 hour round-trips are also available and include bus stops in the Navajo Indian Reservation, a four- to five-hour float down a stretch of the Colorado River, and a picnic-style lunch; for information, call 520-638-2401.

Fishing

Arizona state fishing licenses are required for any fishing in the park, and trout stamps are required for all trout fishing. These can be obtained at Babbitt's General Store in Grand Canyon Village. For current fees, call 520-638-2262. All park visitors who plan to fish are responsible for knowing and complying with state fishing regulations.

OVERNIGHT STAYS

Lodging and Dining

Reservations for the following hotels, lodges, and cabins in the park can be made by contacting AmFac Parks and Resorts, Inc., 14001 E. Iliff Ave., Suite 600, Aurora, CO 80014; 303-297-2757 (the first six are in Grand Canyon Village, South Rim):

El Tovar Hotel, a historic hotel dating from 1905, open year-round. Rooms and suites, dining room, cocktail lounge, gift shop, and newsstand.

Bright Angel Lodge, open year-round. Rustic rooms and cabins, restaurant, soda fountain, gift shop, newsstand, barber and beauty shops.

Maswik Lodge, open year-round. Rooms, cafeteria, cocktail lounge, gift shop, and newsstand.

Yavapai Lodge, open March through December. Rooms, cafeteria, gift shop, newsstand.

Kachina Lodge, open year-round. Rooms; restaurant nearby.

Thunderbird Lodge, open year-round. Rooms; restaurant nearby.

Grand Canyon Lodge, a historic North Rim lodge, open from May 15 to October 15. Cabins and rooms, dining room, cafeteria, cocktail lounge, and gift shop.

Phantom Ranch, located at the bottom of the canyon, open year-round. Dormitory accommodations, cabins, and dining hall for hikers and mule riders.

Lodging Outside the Park

Accommodations outside the park are located in communities such as Tusayan, Flagstaff, Williams, Cameron, Marble Canyon, Jacob Lake, and Kanab, Utah. Especially during the summer, please consider using these lodgings to help decrease visitor impact on the park.

Campgrounds

The Grand Canyon provides multiple options for campers. Many stay on the North or South Rim, at elevations of between 7,000 and 8,000 feet. The South Rim's Mather (open December through February) and Desert View campgrounds operate on a first-come, first-served basis. Campgrounds fill up almost every day by noon from at least early June to mid-September. Reservations are recommended for Mather from March through December and for the North Rim's group campgrounds. They can be made through the National Park Reservation Service at 800-365-CAMP; see "Camping Reservations" under General Information. Reservations are also recommended for the South Rim's Trailer Village and can be made by contacting the park concessioner at Grand Canyon National Park Lodges, Reservations Office, P.O. Box 699, Grand Canyon, AZ 86023; 520-638-2401.

Water, electrical, and sewage hookups for RVs are available in the park only at Trailer Village, adjacent to Mather Campground. No more than six people are permitted at each Desert View, Mather, and North Rim campsite. Services available at Desert View are snack bar, service station, and evening ranger programs. Mather Campground/Trailer Village has a store, hot showers, laundry, service station, visitor center, post office, evening interpretive programs, and cafeterias and restaurants nearby. North Rim Campground has a camper store, hot showers, laundry, service station, post office, and nearby cafeteria and dining room. Fires are permitted only in the grills at Mather and Desert View campgrounds.

Backcountry Camping

Backcountry camping on the rims and in the canyon is allowed year-round in many parts of the park with a free backcountry permit. However, permits are limited in the number issued and are quickly reserved once they are made available. Permits may be obtained up to four months in advance from the Backcountry Office. For full details, request a copy of the Backcountry Trip Planner by calling 520-638-7888 or by writing to the park's Backcountry Office. Same-day permits are sometimes available in person at that office. No open fires are permitted within the canyon; canned heat or portable stoves must be used for cooking.

▲ *Colorado River, Toroweap Point, Grand Canyon National Park, Arizona*

FLORA AND FAUNA (Partial Listings)

Mammals: bighorn sheep, mule deer, mountain lion, coyote, bobcat, gray fox, porcupine, ringtail, striped and spotted skunks, chipmunk, golden-mantled ground squirrel, rock squirrel, red squirrel, and two closely related species of tassle-eared squirrels: the Abert squirrel on the South Rim and the white-tailed Kaibab squirrel on the North Rim.

Birds: golden eagle, peregrine falcon, great horned owl, wild turkey, broad-tailed and black-chinned hummingbirds, white-throated swift, violet-green swallow, Clark's nutcracker, scrub and Steller's jays, raven, mountain chickadee, plain titmouse, white-breasted and pygmy nuthatches, canyon and rock wrens, hermit thrush, western and mountain bluebirds, Townsend's solitaire, a number of warblers including Lucy's and black-throated gray, western tanager, black-headed grosbeak, dark-eyed and gray-headed juncoes, and red crossbills.

Amphibians and Reptiles: Great Basin spadefoot toad, red-spotted toad, canyon treefrog, chuckwalla, short-horned lizard, western collared lizard, side-blotched lizard, western whiptail, gopher snake, long-nosed snake, kingsnake, and the venomous western rattlesnake. One of three subspecies of the latter inhabiting the park is the pinkish Grand Canyon rattler that lives at lower elevations of the canyon.

Trees, Shrubs, Flowers, and Ferns:
Engelmann spruce, blue spruce, and white fir (all on the North Rim), Douglas fir, ponderosa and pinyon pines, Utah juniper, Gambel oak, quaking aspen, Fremont cottonwood, bigtooth maple, boxelder, western redbud, catclaw, mesquite, Apache plume, cliffrose, mountain mahogany, fernbush, rabbitbrush, Utah serviceberry, banana yucca, Utah agave, and ephedra. The most common species of brightly flowering cacti are barrel, fishhook, Whipple cholla, beavertail, pancake pear, Engelmann's prickly pear, plains prickly pear, and claret-cup hedgehog. The numerous wildflowers include segolily, sacred datura, stemless townsendia, sulfur flower, golden and Colorado columbines, red and yellow monkeyflowers, gold-aster, crownbeard, globemallow, skyrocket gilia, paintbrush, several penstemons, cardinal flower, spreading phlox, alpine shootingstar, Canada violet asters, blue flax, iris, gentian, lupine, and larkspur. A few of the ferns are maidenhair, several of the lip ferns, woodsia, wavy cloak, and bracken.

RELATED PRIVATE ORGANIZATIONS

The Grand Canyon Association is a nonprofit corporation that supports visitor-related activities in the national park. It operates bookstores in the park and receives other revenues from donations and membership fees. Founded in 1932, it has donated more than $6 million to the National Park Service for interpretation, research, maintenance, equipment, restoration, and renovations at the canyon. For more information, contact the association at P.O. Box 399, Grand Canyon, AZ 86023; 520-638-2481.

Grand Canyon Trust is a registered nonprofit membership organization that advocates responsible conservation of the natural resources of the Colorado Plateau. For more information, contact the trust at Route 4, Box 718, Flagstaff, AZ 86001; 520-774-7488.

Grand Canyon Field Institute offers educational courses in such areas as wilderness skills, human history, geology, storytelling, art, writing, and photography. College credit is available for some courses. For further information, contact the institute at P.O. Box 399, Grand Canyon, AZ 86023.

NEARBY POINTS OF INTEREST

The region surrounding Grand Canyon National Park offers a tremendous amount of exciting natural and cultural attractions that can be enjoyed as day trips or overnight excursions. Wupatki, Sunset Crater, Walnut Canyon, Canyon de Chelly, Navajo, Pipe Spring, Montezuma Castle and Tuzigoot national monuments; Zion and Bryce Canyon national parks; and Glen Canyon and Lake Mead national recreation areas are some of

▲ *Mt. Hayden, viewed from Point Imperial, Grand Canyon National Park, Arizona*

the many national park units within a day's drive of the park. The Kaibab National Forest adjoins the park to the north and south. Within the national forest district to the north are the Saddle Mountain Wilderness and Kanab Creek Wilderness (both adjoining the park).

To the north of the Grand Canyon, on U.S. Bureau of Land Management (BLM) lands, are the Paria Canyon-Vermilion Cliffs Wilderness, the Dominguez-Escalante Interpretive Site, Mt.

Trumbull Wilderness, Mt. Logan Wilderness, Grand Wash Cliffs Wilderness, Paiute Wilderness, Beaver Dam Mountains Wilderness, Virgin River Gorge Recreation Area, and the Dutchman Trail for Mountain Bikes. Information regarding these and other places on the Arizona Strip can be obtained by contacting the BLM's Arizona Strip District Office, 390 North 3050 East, St. George, UT 84770; 801-673-3545.

Big Bend National Park

▲ *Prickly pear cactus overlooking the Rio Grande, San Vicente Canyon*

Big Bend National Park

P.O. Box 129
Big Bend National Park, TX 79834-0129
915-477-2251

The Big Bend area of west Texas is one of the most magnificent desert areas of the Southwest. This remote and beautiful land consisting of vast desert, rugged mountains, and sheer-walled river canyons is named for the sharp bend in the Rio Grande. The river, which is the international boundary between the United States and Mexico, flows for 118 miles along the southern edge of the park. The park's topographic variety supports a remarkable diversity of flora and fauna, including a thousand plant species (a few found nowhere else in the world) and more than 400 species of birds. The scenic beauty, ecological richness, and colorful human history make 801,000-acre Big Bend National Park an outstanding national treasure.

The park was established by act of Congress in 1944 and was designated a Biosphere Reserve in 1981. The park's Mariscal and Boquillas canyons are also part of the 191-mile-long Rio Grande Wild & Scenic River, which extends downstream from the park on the U.S. side of the Rio Grande to the Terrell-Val County line.

OUTSTANDING FEATURES

Among the many outstanding features of the park are the following: Sotol Vista Overlook, which offers an excellent view of the surrounding desert and mountains; Castolon, an old army fort that protected area residents from bandits during the 1914-18 troubles with Mexico; Santa Elena Canyon Overlook, a spot providing a grand view of the lower end of this sheer-walled, Rio Grande-carved gash through 1,500-foot-high Mesa de Anguila; Boquillas Canyon Overlook, which offers a view into the mouth of this deep Rio Grande gorge that cuts through the massive Sierra del Carmen Range; the Chisos Mountains, the park's central feature that includes the Chisos Basin, a scenic valley from which the Lost Mine Trail leads hikers into the jagged heights of Lost Mine Ridge up to the 7,835-foot-high summit of Emory Peak and on to the South Rim; Pine Canyon, an area at the eastern base of the Chisos where water has created an ecologically rich oasis; and Fossil Bone Exhibit and Sam Nail Ranch, which contains the remains of windmills and a ranch house.

PRACTICAL INFORMATION

When to Go

The park is open daily year-round. Mid- to late autumn, winter, and early to mid-spring are the most pleasant seasons to visit because of the predominantly mild temperatures. Especially after winters of sufficient rainfall, spring provides magnificent displays of wildflowers, including vast expanses of bluebonnets. Spring is also especially outstanding for birdwatching. Summer is intensely hot, with temperatures often surpassing 100 degrees at lower elevations.

How to Get There

By Car: To the north entrance: from U.S. Route 90 at Marathon, drive south 40 miles on U.S. Route 385 and then south 28 miles through the park to the main visitor center at Panther Junction. To the west entrance: from U.S. Route 90 at Alpine, drive south 78 miles on State Route 118 and then east 26 miles through the park to the main visitor center at Panther Junction.

By Air: Southwest Airlines (800-435-9792) and other carriers serve San Antonio International, El Paso International, and Midland-Odessa airports.

By Train: Amtrak (800-872-7245) has stops at Sanderson and Alpine.

By Bus: Greyhound Lines (800-231-2222) has stops at Alpine.

Fees and Permits

Entrance fees are $10 per car or $5 per per-

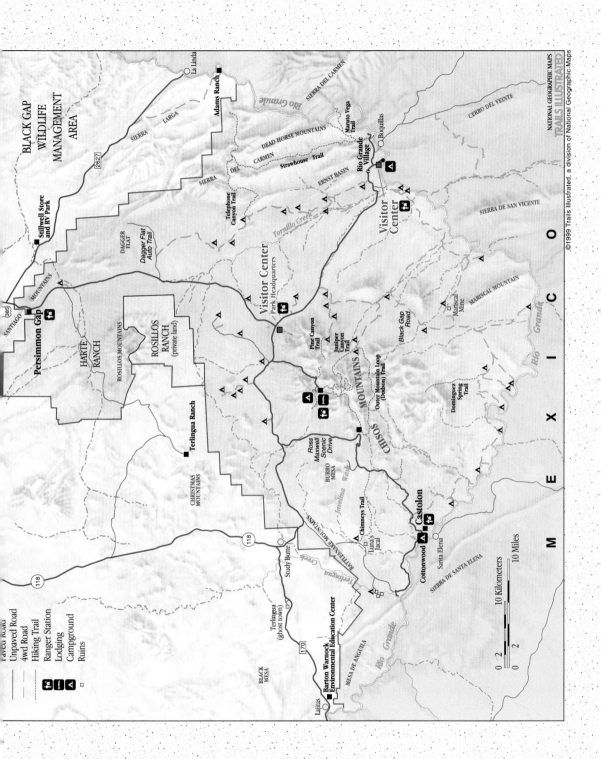

Paved Road
Unpaved Road
4wd Road
Hiking Trail
Ranger Station
Lodging
Campground
Ruins

BLACK GAP
WILDLIFE
MANAGEMENT
AREA

2627

Stillwell Store
and RV Park

SIERRA LARGA

La Linda

Adams Ranch

SIERRA DEL CARMEN

Rio Grande

SIERRA DEL

DEAD HORSE MOUNTAINS

CARMEN

Strawhouse Trail

SIERRA DEL

Maruto Vega Trail

Boquillas

Telephone
Canyon Trail

ERNST BASIN

Rio Grande
Village

Tornillo Creek

DAGGER
FLAT

Dagger Flat
Auto Trail

Visitor Center
Park Headquarters

Visitor
Center

SIERRA DE SAN VICENTE

385

SANTIAGO

MOUNTAINS

Persimmon Gap

HARTE
RANCH

ROSILLOS MOUNTAINS

ROSILLOS
RANCH
(private land)

Pine Canyon
Trail

Juniper
Canyon Trail

Black Gap
Road

Mariscal
Mine

MARISCAL MOUNTAIN

Outer Mountain Loop
(Dodson) Trail

CHISOS

MOUNTAINS

Terlingua Ranch

Dominguez
Spring
Trail

Rio

Grande

Ross
Maxwell
Scenic
Drive

CHRISTMAS
MOUNTAINS

BURRO
MESA

Javelina Wash

Chimneys Trail

Castolon

Luna's
Jacal

Cottonwood

Castolon

118

Study Butte

BATTLESNAKE MOUNTAINS

Santa Elena

Terlingua Creek

SIERRA DE SANTA ELENA

Terlingua
(ghost town)

170

BLACK
MESA

Barton Warnock
Environmental Education Center

MESA DE ANGUILA

Rio

Grande

Lajitas

M   E   X   I   C   O

CERRO DEL VEINTE

NATIONAL GEOGRAPHIC MAPS
TRAILS ILLUSTRATED

©1999 Trails Illustrated, a division of National Geographic Maps

10 Kilometers

10 Miles

0   2   10

0   2   10

◀ *Pinyon pine and agave, Chisos Mountains, Big Bend National Park, Texas*

son on foot, bicycle, or motorcycle or by bus; passes are valid for seven consecutive days. Free permits, available at visitor centers, are required for backcountry camping and for boat use in river float trips.

Visitor Centers

Panther Junction: open daily year-round 8 a.m.-6 p.m. Interpretive exhibits and programs, publications, maps, driving tour guides, a hiker's trail guide, schedules of interpretive programs and other activities.

Rio Grande Village: open mid-October through early May, 8:30 a.m.-4 p.m.

Chisos Basin: open 8 a.m.-3:30 p.m., as staffing allows.

Persimmon Gap: open 8 a.m.-4 p.m., as staffing allows.

Facilities

Available are lodge, restaurant, service stations, groceries, camping supplies, hot showers, laundry, and post office.

Handicapped Accessibility

Restrooms, visitor centers, and several trails are wheelchair accessible.

Medical Services

No medical services are available in the park. A clinic and paramedic service are available at Terlingua, 25 miles from the main visitor center. The nearest hospital is in Alpine, 104 miles from the main visitor center.

Pets

Pets are allowed on leashes, but not on trails or in public buildings. Horseback riding is permitted in most areas.

Safety and Regulations

For your safety and enjoyment and for the protection of the park, please follow these regulations and suggestions:

- Remember that, from mid-spring to mid-autumn, temperatures often approach or exceed 100 degrees and water and fuel are available at only widely separated places within the park, so check supplies before you leave facilities.

- Be informed and well equipped—especially with a generous supply of water—before running the river or setting out on hikes. (On a hot day's trek, a hiker can consume as much as a gallon of water).

- Do not drink river water; drink water at springs only after treating it.

- Sun protection is highly advised, and it is a good idea to carry tweezers when hiking if needed to remove small spines.

- Keep alert for rattlesnakes.

- Great care should be taken when wading or swimming in the Rio Grande, as there are deceptively strong currents, submerged snags and rocks, and sudden drop-offs.

- Avoid camping in arroyos or washes due to the potential of flash flooding. Building wood or ground fires is prohibited as the fire danger is often extremely high.

- Stay on established trails to prevent erosion and slides, and to avoid the risk of getting lost. Because of the high fire danger, smoking on trails is not allowed.

- Motor vehicles must stay on established roads.

- Firearms are strictly prohibited in the park.

- Remember that it is illegal to feed, pet, hunt, capture, or otherwise disturb wildlife in any way. Trees and other plantlife including wildflowers are not to be cut down or picked.

The National Park Service asks that visitors not litter the park. Remember the excellent slogan to "leave only footprints" as a guide to help protect this national park.

ACTIVITIES

Options include hiking, birdwatching, spring wildflower identification, photography, picnicking, backpacking, camping, river-running by raft and canoe, horseback riding, interpretive programs, nature seminars, and catfish fishing

in the river (for which a license is not required). Further information is available in the park's newspaper, *El Paisano*.

Hiking Trails

Among Big Bend's many hiking trails are: **Santa Elena Canyon Trail**, an .8-mile trail providing a short, easy hike into the lower end of this awesome, sheer-walled Rio Grande gorge in 1,500-foot-high Mesa de Anguila; the opposite side of the canyon is in Mexico; **Boquillas Canyon Trail**, a .7-mile hike into the upper end of this deep canyon carved through the Sierra del Carmen Mountains; the opposite side is in Mexico; **Pine Canyon Trail**, a delightful two-mile trail into the oasis of Pine Canyon at the eastern base of the Chisos Mountains; the trailhead is at the end of the unpaved, high-clearance, four-wheel-drive road that leads to the Pine Canyon primitive camp site; **Lost Mine Trail**, a 2.4-mile trail winding up from a point along the road that leads into the river basin and then to a spectacular ridgetop overlook and view of Lost Mine Peak; **Pinnacles Trail**, a trail leading hikers from the basin up to the high country of the Chisos Mountains: from the basin to the highest summit, 7,835-foot Emory Peak, is 3.5 miles on this trail and a mile on the steep Emory Peak Trail; from the Basin to Laguna Meadows is 3.5 miles; from the basin to Boot Spring is 4.8 miles; and from the basin to the South Rim is 6.3 miles; horseback riding is not permitted on most trails in the Chisos, but is allowed on the Laguna Meadows Trail, which also leads to the South Rim; **Juniper Canyon Trail**, a 6.2-mile trail up Juniper Canyon, climbing steeply into the Chisos and connecting with trails from the basin; the trailhead is at the end of the unpaved, high-clearance, four-wheel-drive road at the Juniper Canyon primitive camp site; and **Chimneys Trail**, a 7.6-mile desert trail running east-west between a point on the road to Santa Elena Canyon and the Chimneys West primitive campsite.

For further information on these and other trails and their condition, visitors are encouraged to contact park staff at any of the visitor centers. It is critically important to carry and drink sufficient water on hikes. (On a hot day's trek, a hiker can consume as much as a gallon of water).

▲ *Blind prickly pear and basalt boulders, Big Bend National Park, Texas*

OVERNIGHT STAYS

Lodging and Dining

Chisos Mountain Lodge, which also has a dining room and gift shop, accepts reservations for overnight accommodations; contact National Park Concessions, Inc., Big Bend National Park, TX 79834; 915-477-2291. Especially in spring and autumn, there is great demand for lodgings, so making reservations far in advance is highly recommended.

Campgrounds

Campgrounds are available in the Chisos Basin (5,400 feet elevation) and down by the river, at Rio Grande Village (1,850 feet elevation) and at Cottonwood (2,100 feet elevation) near Castolon. They are open year-round, and camp sites are available on a first-come, first-served basis. Rio Grande Village Trailer Park provides water, sewer, and electrical hookups for RVs. Visitors towing trailers longer than 20 feet or driving motorhomes longer than 24 feet are discouraged from trying to reach the Basin Campground because the access road up Green Gulch is narrow, winding, and has a steep 15 percent grade. Group camping is available year-round at the Basin (three to 12 people per site), Cottonwood (ten to 30 people per site), and Rio Grande Village (up to 40 people per site). Reservations are required; contact the park up to 90 days in advance. Campgrounds are for organized groups only.

FLORA AND FAUNA (Partial Listings)

Mammals: Carmen Mountains whitetail deer in the Chisos Mountains and mule deer on the desert, pronghorn, mountain lion, coyote, gray fox, javelina (peccary), beaver, ringtail, antelope and ground squirrels, and skunks (hog-nosed, hooded, spotted, and striped).

Birds: pied-billed grebe, green-winged teal, great blue heron, red-tailed and zone-tailed hawk, golden eagle, scaled quail, band-tailed pigeon, white-winged and mourning doves, roadrunner, owls (great horned, elf, screech, and flammulated), white-throated swift, at least a half-dozen hummingbirds (including Lucifer, broad-tailed, and blue-throated), belted kingfisher, acorn and ladder-backed woodpeckers, vermilion flycatcher, Mexican jay, raven, black-crested titmouse, verdin, bushtit, wrens (Bewick's, cactus, canyon, and rock), curve-billed thrasher, hermit thrush, Townsend's solitaire, phainopepla, Hutton's vireo, numerous warblers (such as orange-crowned, Colima, Grace's, yellow, yellow-rumped, Townsend's, yellowthroat, Wilson's, and American and painted redstarts), orioles (Bullock's, hooded, and Scott's), summer and hepatic tanagers, cardinal, pyrrhuloxia, black-headed and blue grosbeaks, varied and painted buntings, towhees (green-tailed, rufous-sided, and canyon), and a number of sparrows, including rufous-crowned, black-throated, black-chinned, white-crowned, and Lincoln's.

Amphibians and Reptiles: canyon treefrog, Rio Grande leopard frog, red-spotted and spadefoot toads, Texas banded gecko, lizards (collared, crevice spiny, tree, horned, side-blotched, and greater earless), rattlesnakes (black-tailed, rock, and western diamondback), Trans-Pecos copperhead,

Mexican kingsnake, blackneck garter snake, striped whipsnake, and western coachwhip.

Trees, Shrubs, and Flowers: Among the park's trees are Arizona cypress, alligator and drooping junipers, Mexican pinyon and ponderosa pines, Douglas fir, Texas madrone, Mexican black walnut, quaking aspen, cottonwood, bigtooth maple, oaks (gray, Graves, Gambel's, Emory, and Chisos red), fragrant ash, Mexican redbud, honey and screwbean mesquites, desert hackberry, desert-willow, and the riverbank exotic, tamarisk. Shrubs include mountain sage (salvia), Texas mountain-laurel (mescalbean), Mexican buckeye, desert ceanothus, New Mexico dalea, forestiera, catclaw, white-thorn, and other acacias, catclaw-mimosa, ceniza, creosotebush, tarbush, little-leaf sumac, ratany, scarlet bouvardia, ephedra, mountain mahogany, ocotillo, candelilla (wax-plant), Torrey (Spanish-dagger) and Thompson yuccas, sotol, nolina, false-agave, and maguey, Big Bend, and lechuguilla agaves. The latter is a key indicator species of the Chihuahuan Desert. Of the many cacti, there are claretcup hedgehog, button, Corey, eagle's-claw, pitaya (strawberry cactus) and purple pitaya, rainbow, Texas pride, cane cholla, and Engelmann, long-spine, and blind prickly pears. The multitudes of wildflowers include Big Bend bluebonnet, Havard pentstemon, Wright verbena, Chisos prickly poppy, bladder-pod, Indian paintbrush, longspur columbine, cardinal-flower, monkeyflower, yellow trumpet-flower, phacelia, prickle-leaf and Stewart gilias, Berlandier flax, orange caltrop, hairy resurrection plant, and golden crownbeard.

NEARBY POINTS OF INTEREST

The areas surrounding Big Bend offer some exciting natural and historical attractions that can be enjoyed as day trips or overnight excursions. Fort Davis National Historic Site and the Davis Mountains State Park are about 125 miles north on State Route 118. Amistad National Recreation Area is due east near Del Rio, and Chamizal National Memorial is about 320 miles northwest in El Paso. Guadalupe Mountains National Park is to the northwest, adjoining the New Mexico state line, in west Texas; and Carlsbad Caverns National Park is nearby, over the line in New Mexico.

CANYON DE CHELLY NATIONAL MONUMENT

▲ *Spider Rock and Canyon de Chelly*

Canyon de Chelly National Monument

P.O. Box 588
Chinle, AZ 86503
520-674-5500

One of the Southwest's most fascinating national monuments, Canyon de Chelly (pronounced "deh SHAY" and derived from a Navajo word, Tseyi, meaning "among the canyon" or "among the rocks") is located on the Navajo Indian Reservation in northeast Arizona. With its spectacular, sheer-walled canyons and numerous ruins of prehistoric Anasazi pueblo dwellings nestled at the base of towering cliffs or perched in shallow caves, this monument typifies the colorful Southwestern Indian canyon country. Adding to the natural splendor and prehistoric cultural heritage are present-day Navajo Indians, several hundred of whom live in these canyons from May to October tending flocks of sheep, raising crops of corn, beans, squash, and melons, and cultivating peach orchards. A few Navajos lead interpretive jeep tours for visitors. There are three main canyons within the 83,840-acre monument: 27-mile-long Canyon de Chelly, 18-mile Canyon del Muerto (named for the massacre of Spaniards there in 1805), and ten-mile Monument Canyon.

The monument was established in 1931. Unlike nearly all other National Park System units, the U.S. government does not own the land within the boundaries of this national monument. Rather, management is carried out jointly by the Navajo Nation and the National Park Service. Visitors to the monument are asked to be respectful of the Navajo people and of their property and privacy.

of white-plastered pueblo wall in the upper part of the ruin; and **Spider Rock**, an 800-foot-tall, slender sandstone spire that rises boldly from the floor of the canyon at the junction of Canyon de Chelly and Monument Canyon. Notable features in Canyon del Muerto include: **Antelope House**, which is named for its colorful Navajo paintings of antelope dating from the 1830s; and **Mummy Cave**, which was occupied from A.D. 300 to the late 1200s and contains the ruins of the largest and one of the most spectacular cliff dwellings in the monument. Panels of pictographs, petroglyphs, drawings, and diagrams may be seen scattered here and there on sections of canyon walls.

Among outstanding overlooks on the 22-mile *South Rim Drive* (Navajo Route 7) of Canyon de Chelly are the following (from northwest to southeast): **Junction Overlook**, which is at the junction of Canyon de Chelly and Canyon del Muerto; **White House Overlook**, a view across Canyon de Chelly to White House Ruin and from which the White House Trail leads hikers into and across the 500-foot-deep canyon on a two-hour hike; **Sliding House Overlook**, which offers a view of Sliding House Ruin across the canyon and from which it is occasionally possible to watch the sun set in the west and the full moon to rise in the east at virtually the same moment; and **Spider Rock Overlook**, a spectacular view of this awesome rock formation at the junction of Canyon de Chelly and Monument Canyon, reached by a short path.

From southwest to northeast, among the main overlooks along the *North Rim* (Navajo Route 64) of Canyon del Muerto are: **Ledge Ruin Overlook**, a spot just upcanyon from the junction of Canyon de Chelly and Canyon del Muerto; **Antelope House Overlook**, which offers a grand view of the canyon; and **Mummy Cave Overlook**, a view across the canyon to Mummy Cave.

OUTSTANDING FEATURES

Among the many outstanding features in Canyon de Chelly are: **White House Ruin**, a 175-room masonry pueblo which was built beginning around A.D. 1066 and occupied until the 1200s; its name comes from a section

ACTIVITIES

Options include hiking (except on the White House Ruin Trail, visitors must be accompanied by a ranger or authorized Navajo guide), driving to scenic overlooks along the South and

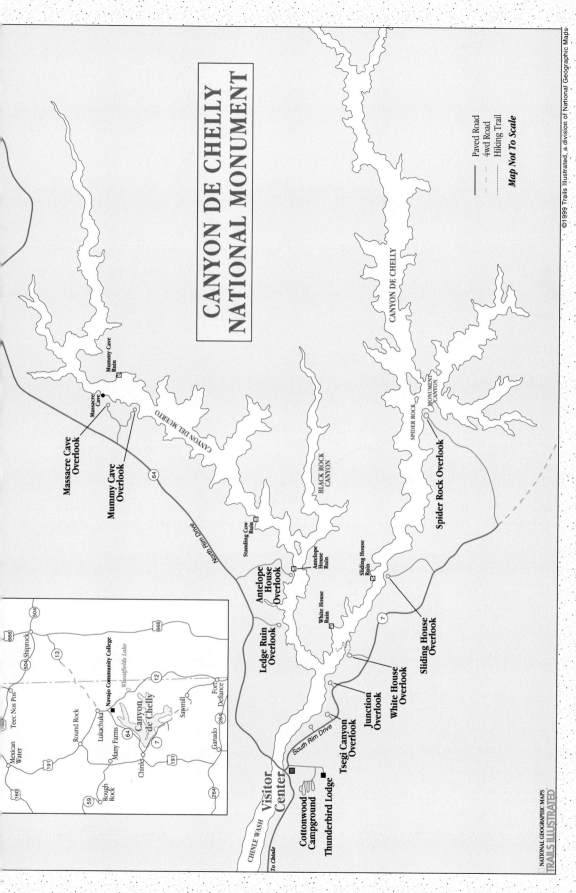

CANYON DE CHELLY NATIONAL MONUMENT

Paved Road
4wd Road
Hiking Trail

Map Not To Scale

©1999 Trails Illustrated, a division of National Geographic Maps

Massacre Cave Overlook

Mummy Cave Overlook

Massacre Cave

Mummy Cave Ruin

CANYON DEL MUERTO

North Rim Drive

64

Standing Cow Ruin

Antelope House Overlook

Antelope House Ruin

BLACK ROCK CANYON

Ledge Ruin Overlook

White House Ruin

7

Sliding House Ruin

Sliding House Overlook

CANYON DE CHELLY

SPIDER ROCK

Spider Rock

MONUMENT CANYON

Spider Rock Overlook

Junction Overlook

White House Overlook

Tsegi Canyon Overlook

South Rim Drive

CHINLE WASH

To Chinle

Visitor Center

Cottonwood Campground

Thunderbird Lodge

NATIONAL GEOGRAPHIC MAPS
TRAILS ILLUSTRATED

504

666

504 Shiprock

13

504

Teec Nos Pos

Mexican Water

160

191

59

Rough Rock

Round Rock

Many Farms

Lukachukai

Navajo Community College

Wheatfields Lake

12

Canyon de Chelly

64

7

Sawmill

Fort Defiance

Ganado

264

191

Chinle

264

W. A. Woodard Memorial Library

North Rim routes, horseback riding, photography, rock-art viewing, picnicking, camping, visitor center interpretive exhibits and programs, and pictograph viewing. For jeep tours, call 520-674-5841/5842. Further information is available in the park's newspaper, *Canyon Overlook*.

PRACTICAL INFORMATION

When to Go

The monument is open year-round, 8 a.m.-5 p.m. (6 p.m. in summer).

160 at Tuba City, drive east 119 miles on State Route 264 (through the Hopi Indian Reservation) and north 30 miles on U.S. Route 191 to Chinle.

By Air: There are flights from Phoenix to Flagstaff Pulliam Airport (520-556-1234) and Page Municipal Airport (602-645-2494).

By Train: Amtrak (800-872-7245) has stops in Flagstaff, Winslow, and Gallup.

By Bus: Greyhound Lines (800-231-2222) has stops in Phoenix and Flagstaff.

Fees and Permits

There is no entrance fee. Permits are required for hiking and four-wheel driving in the canyons (both with guides only).

Visitor Center

Canyon de Chelly Visitor Center, at the junction of the South and North Rim drives at the west end of the monument: open daily 8 a.m.-5 p.m. (6 p.m. in summer). Interpretive exhibits, programs, publications, and other information.

Handicapped Accessibility

Some overlooks in the monument are accessible.

Medical Services

Only emergency first aid is available in the park. The closest hospital is in Chinle, just west of the monument.

Safety and Regulations

For your safety and enjoyment and for the protection of the park, please follow these regulations and suggestions:

- Visitors should take care not to leave valuables unattended even in locked motor vehicles, when going for even short walks.

- Quicksand, deep dry sand, flash floods, cliffs, and loose rocks can cause hazardous conditions.

How to Get There

By Car: From I-40 at Chambers, drive north 74 miles on U.S. Route 191 to Chinle, at the west end of the monument. From U.S. Route 160 near Mexican Hat, drive south 62 miles on U.S. Route 191 to Chinle. From U.S. Route

43

- Do not pick up or remove any cultural objects, climb or sit on any walls of prehistoric pueblo ruins, enter any Navajo hogan, or take photographs of the Navajo people without their consent.
- Alcohol is not allowed on the Navajo Reservation.

OVERNIGHT STAYS

Lodging and Dining

The *Thunderbird Lodge* in the gateway community of Chinle has rooms available year-round; for reservations, contact the lodge at Box 548, Chinle, AZ 86503; 520-674-5841/5842. The lodge has a restaurant.

Lodging is also available nearby at the Holiday Inn (520-674-5000) and Best Western (520-674-5875).

Camping

The cottonwood-shaded Cottonwood Campground is located near the junction of Canyon de Chelly and Canyon del Muerto. It is open year-round on a first-come, first-served basis. The campground has 104 sites and two group sites (available April through October for groups of 15-25 people). Reservations, required for group camping, are made by contacting the monument headquarters. No RVs are permitted in the group sites; and there is a five-day limit per visit, 14 days annually.

Backcountry Camping

Backcountry camping is permitted only with a Navajo guide, as this is Navajo Indian land and many residents live within the canyons.

FLORA AND FAUNA (Partial Listings)

Mammals: mule deer, coyote, gray fox, bobcat, badger, raccoon, ringtail, porcupine, striped skunk, blacktail jackrabbit, desert cottontail, Abert squirrel, and cliff chipmunk.

Birds: wild turkey, red-tailed hawk, golden eagle, great horned owl, black-chinned hummingbird, Say's phoebe, white-throated swift, violet-green and cliff swallows, raven, scrub and pinyon jays, plain titmouse, rock and canyon wrens, western and mountain bluebirds, yellow-rumped and black-throated gray warblers, black-headed grosbeak, northern oriole, western tanager, and rufous-sided towhee.

Reptiles: canyon tree, collared, and horned lizards.

Trees, Shrubs, and Flowers: ponderosa and pinyon pines, Douglas fir, Utah juniper, Gambel oak, cottonwood, mountain mahogany, Utah serviceberry, cliffrose, ephedra, tamarisk, prickly pear and cane cholla cacti, narrow-leaved yucca, sacred datura, penstemon, gilia, globemallow, sunflowers, and asters.

NEARBY POINTS OF INTEREST

Canyon de Chelly is part of the "Grand Circle," which is the largest concentration of national parks, monuments, and recreation areas anywhere on Earth. If your schedule allows, plan to visit other outstanding National Park System units in the surrounding area, such as Hubbell Trading Post National Historic Site, Navajo National Monument, Wupatki National Monument, and Grand Canyon National Park.

44

CARLSBAD CAVERNS NATIONAL PARK

▲ Colorful stalactites, Papoose Room

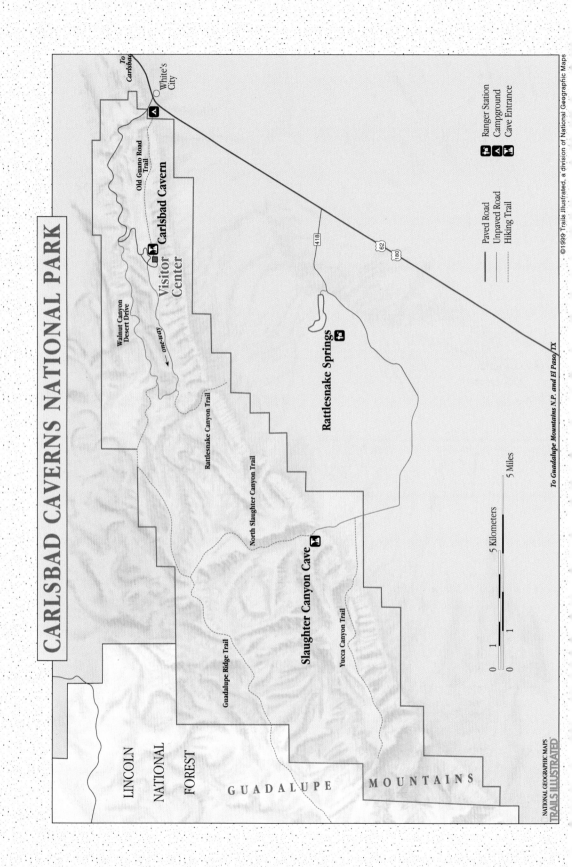

CARLSBAD CAVERNS NATIONAL PARK

To Carlsbad

White's City

Old Guano Road Trail

Carlsbad Cavern

Visitor Center

Walnut Canyon Desert Drive

one-way

Rattlesnake Canyon Trail

Rattlesnake Springs

North Slaughter Canyon Trail

418

62
180

Slaughter Canyon Cave

Guadalupe Ridge Trail

Yucca Canyon Trail

LINCOLN

NATIONAL

FOREST

GUADALUPE   MOUNTAINS

Ranger Station
Campground
Cave Entrance

Paved Road
Unpaved Road
Hiking Trail

0   1   5 Kilometers
0   1   5 Miles

NATIONAL GEOGRAPHIC MAPS
TRAILS ILLUSTRATED

To Guadalupe Mountains N.P. and El Paso, TX

©1999 Trails Illustrated, a division of National Geographic Maps

Carlsbad Caverns National Park

**3225 National Parks Highway
Carlsbad, NM 88220-5354
505-785-2232**

Deep below the surface of the Chihuahuan Desert in southeast New Mexico lies a fantasy underworld of incredible proportions. One of the deepest, largest, and most ornate caverns ever found, this spectacular honeycomb of chambers contains more than 30 miles of passageways, with an endless variety of glistening mineral formations. At its deepest, this cave is more than 1,000 feet below the surface. Originally called "Bat Cave" for its hour-long cyclone of bats emerging each evening at dusk, this natural wonder is an amazing subterranean creation of which we have only seen the beginning.

The 46,766-acre park also protects at least 70 other separate cave systems. One of those, discovered in 1986, is Lechuguilla Cave, which is already known to extend over 80 miles and, at 1,566 feet, is the deepest known cave in North America. Because of the hazardous climbing conditions and extremely delicate gypsum formations, that cave is open only to qualified researchers who are skilled climbers.

The area was proclaimed a national monument in 1923 and established as a national park in 1930. Much of the park was designated a wilderness area in 1978. Yet the challenges continue. NPCA and the National Park Service strongly and successfully opposed a recent plan to drill for natural gas on adjacent federal land near the park's northern boundary, close to Lechuguilla Cave. NPCA also continues to recommend that the magnificent 25,000-acre Guadalupe Escarpment area be added to the park and to push for removal of the underground lunchroom that is impairing some of Carlsbad Cavern's irreplaceable formations.

OUTSTANDING FEATURES

Among the many outstanding features of the park are the following: **Carlsbad Cavern's Green Lake Room**, which contains a pool amid an array of stalagmites, including the exquisite column known as the Veiled Statue; the **King's Palace**, one of the most ornate cave rooms in the world; the **Queen's Chamber**, which features elegant stone draperies and rare helictites; the **Papoose Room**, an area with suspended draperies of colorful stalactites; the **Hall of Giants**, which contains such awesome formations as the 62-foot-tall stalagmite called the Giant Dome and the 42-foot-tall Twin Domes; the **Big Room,** the second largest room ever discovered, measuring 1,800 feet long by 1,100 feet wide; **New Cave**, an "unimproved" cave that may be viewed by flashlight in a ranger-guided tour in scenic Slaughter Canyon; several scenic desert canyons, including **Slaughter Canyon** and **Rattlesnake Canyon**, where visitors may explore some of this fascinating semi-arid desert by trail; and ecologically rich **Rattlesnake Springs**, a riparian oasis just off the road (County Route 418) to Slaughter Canyon in a small separate park unit that is popular for birdwatching.

PRACTICAL INFORMATION

When to Go

The park is open daily year-round, except Christmas Day. Tours of New Cave are given daily in summer and on weekends the rest of the year. Cool cave temperatures (mid-50s year-round) draw crowds in summer. The desert blooms in the spring, and the 300,000 Mexican free-tail bats fly out of Carlsbad Cavern's natural entrance at dusk from April through October.

How to Get There

By Car: From Carlsbad, drive southwest 20 miles on U.S. Route 62/180 to White's City,

49

▲ *Big Room, Carlsbad Caverns National Park, New Mexico*

and then less than a mile on State Route 7 to the entrance, from which it is about a 15-minute drive on up to the visitor center. From El Paso, Texas, drive east 143 miles on U.S. 62/180 (passing through part of Guadalupe Mountains National Park) to White's City and the turnoff to the park.

By Air: Mesa Airlines (800-637-2247) provides shuttle flights from Albuquerque to Cavern City Air Terminal at Carlsbad.

By Train: Amtrak (800-872-7245) has stops in Albuquerque and El Paso.

By Bus: Greyhound Lines (800-231-2222) has stops in Carlsbad.

Fees and Permits

For Carlsbad Cavern, fees are $6.50 per person, ages 16-62, and $3.25 per person, ages 6-15. For New Cave, fees are $15 per person, ages 16-62; $7.50 per person, ages 6-15; and under 6 not permitted. Reservations are required and can be made at the visitor center or by calling the park. Free permits, available at the visitor center, are required for backcountry camping. All fees are subject to change; contact the park for current fees.

Visitor Center

Carlsbad Caverns Visitor Center: open daily 8 a.m.-5:30 p.m. (to 7 p.m. in summer). Interpretive exhibits, programs, bookstore, cave tour tickets, talks, tours, and first aid.

Facilities

Available are a restaurant, gift shop, kennel, and nursery for small children. Other facilities are available in White's City and Carlsbad.

Handicapped Accessibility

Most of the Big Room Route (Red Tour) is accessible, as are the visitor center, Bat Flight Amphitheater, restrooms, and the Rattlesnake Springs picnic area.

Pets

Pets are not permitted in caves or the backcountry. A kennel is available at the visitor center.

Safety and Regulations

For your safety and enjoyment and for the protection of the park, please follow these regulations and suggestions:

- Jackets and sturdy, low-heeled, rubber-soled shoes are recommended in caves.
- In desert areas, be alert for rattlesnakes.
- Be careful to avoid contact with cactus spines.
- On hikes, it is important to carry a sufficient supply of water.
- Firearms are strictly forbidden in the park.
- Remember that it is illegal to feed, capture, hunt, or otherwise disturb wildlife, and cutting trees or gathering plantlife is prohibited.

The National Park Service asks that visitors not litter the park. Remember the excellent slogan to "leave only footprints" as a guide to help protect this national park.

ACTIVITIES

Options include ranger-led and self-guided Carlsbad Cavern tours, evening bat-flight programs (spring to fall), ranger-guided flashlight tours of New Cave in Slaughter Canyon, birdwatching, hiking, picnicking, backcountry camping, and nature walks.

Further information is available in the park's newspaper, *Capitan Reef*.

Cave Tours

At *Carlsbad Cavern*, two types of tours are available. The **Blue Tour** is a complete cave walking tour, covering three miles in three hours. This tour begins at the natural entrance, descending in what can be a somewhat strenuous walk, and includes a half-hour stop for lunch and an elevator ride back to the surface. The last Blue Tour departure of the day is at 2 p.m. The **Red Tour** is a partial cave tour, covering 1.25 miles in 1.5 hours. This tour begins with the 755-foot elevator ride to The Big Room, where most types of formations in the cave are visible, and returns to the surface by a 755-foot elevator ride. The last Red Tour departure of the day is at 3:30 p.m.

▲ *"The Chandelier," Big Room, Carlsbad Caverns National Park, New Mexico*

51

Ranger-guided tours of *New Cave* are also available. This two-hour, 1.25-mile, lantern- and flashlight tour includes the Monarch, which at 89 feet is one of the world's tallest columns and the crystal-encrusted Christmas Tree column. This tour is offered daily during the summer and weekends the rest of the year. Be advised that this tour requires a strenuous half-mile hike climbing 500 feet up to the cave entrance and the start of the tour. Sturdy, low-heeled, rubber-soled shoes, a jacket, a supply of water, and a flashlight are essential. Reservations are required. To reach the New Cave, which is in Slaughter Canyon, is about a 45-minute drive from the visitor center.Drive from the park entrance to White's City southwest five miles on U.S. Route 62/180 and then west onto County Route 418 for 11 miles, passing the Rattlesnake Springs unit of the park and onto an unpaved road that ends at a parking area in Slaughter Canyon.

Scenic Drive

The unpaved, 9.5-mile **Walnut Canyon Desert Drive** loops through the park's desert environment. A self-guided interpretive pamphlet of the route is available at the visitor center. The winding drive is not recommended for motor homes and trailers.

Hiking Trails

In addition to a short, self-guided interpretive trail near the visitor center, there are 50 miles of backcountry trails, including the three-mile **Rattlesnake Canyon Trail** that leads from marker #9 on the Walnut Canyon Desert Drive; the six-mile **Yucca Canyon Trail** and 11-mile **Slaughter Canyon Trail**, both of which lead from the Slaughter Canyon road; and the 11.8-mile **Guadalupe Ridge Trail** that provides an overnight trek from Walnut Canyon Desert Drive to the park's west boundary.

Lodging and Dining

No lodging facilities are available in the park, but the nearby communities of White's City and Carlsbad offer overnight accommodations. Dining facilities include a restaurant at the visitor center and at the underground lunchroom.

Backcountry Camping

A free permit is required for backcountry camping. Sites must be a quarter-mile from and out of sight of any park road. As with backcountry hiking, it is important for visitors to be well supplied with water. The nearest campground is outside the park entrance, near White's City.

FLORA AND FAUNA (Partial Listings)

Mammals: mule deer, mountain lion, bobcat, coyote, gray and kit foxes, badger, Mexican free-tail and brown bats, blacktail jack rabbit, desert cottontail, porcupine, raccoon, ringtail, several skunks, and antelope and rock squirrels.

Birds: scaled quail, red-tailed hawk, golden eagle, prairie falcon, great horned owl, roadrunner, black-chinned and broad-tailed hummingbirds, ladder-backed woodpecker, vermilion flycatcher, horned lark, white-throated swift, swallows (cave, rough-winged, and violet-green), raven, scrub jay, plain titmouse, bushtit, verdin, wrens (canyon, rock, cactus, and Bewick's), Crissal and curve-billed thrashers, Townsend's solitaire, western bluebird, warblers (yellowthroat, orange-crowned, and yellow-rumped), yellow-breasted chat, northern and Scott's orioles, hepatic and summer tanagers, sparrows (Cassin's, lark, Brewer's, black-chinned, rufous-crowned, and black-throated), towhees (canyon, rufous-sided, and green-tailed), pyrrhuloxia, and blue grosbeak.

Amphibians and Reptiles: leopard frog, Couch's and western spadefoot toads, red-spotted toad, lizards (collared, crevice spiny, southern prairie, and side-blotched), and a number of snakes, including black-necked garter, coachwhip, desert whipsnake, kingsnake, and western diamondback and black-tailed rattlesnakes.

Trees, Shrubs, and Flowers: pinyon pine, netleaf hackberry, Texas black walnut, western soapberry, cottonwood, mesquite, catclaw acacia, oaks (Gambel's, wavyleaf, and gray), mescalbean, Mexican buckeye, ocotillo, sotol, nolina, yuccas (Torrey, banana, and soaptree), lechuguilla and New Mexico agaves, a number of cacti including Engelmann prickly pear and cane cholla, and globemallow, penstemons, and Indian paintbrush.

NEARBY POINTS OF INTEREST

In the area surrounding Carlsbad Caverns National Park are some exciting natural attractions that can be enjoyed as day trips or overnight excursions. Guadalupe Mountains National Park is directly to the southwest, just over the line in Texas; Lincoln National Forest, adjoining the latter park to the north, is directly to the west and northwest; and White Sands National Monument is about 120 miles to the northwest, near Alamogordo.

GUADALUPE MOUNTAINS NATIONAL PARK

▲ El Capitan at sunset

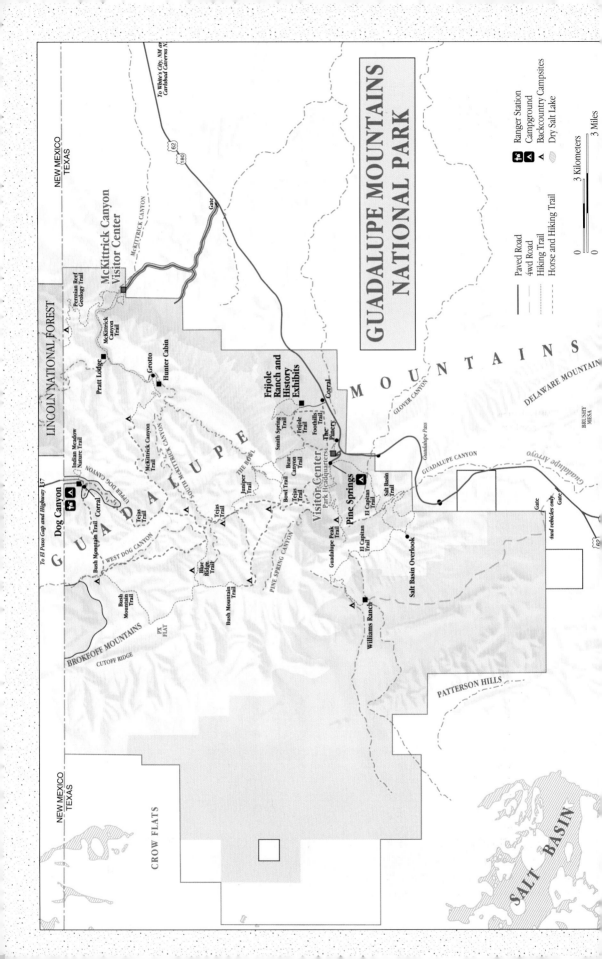

GUADALUPE MOUNTAINS NATIONAL PARK

NEW MEXICO
TEXAS

To White's City, NM and Carlsbad Caverns N.

LINCOLN NATIONAL FOREST

McKittrick Canyon Visitor Center

McKittrick Canyon Trail

Permian Reef Geology Trail

Pratt Lodge

Grotto

Hunter Cabin

Indian Meadow Nature Trail

Dog Canyon

To El Paso Gap and Highway 137

Bush Mountain Trail Corral

UPPER DOG CANYON

WEST DOG CANYON

Tejas Trail

Bush Mountain Trail

McKittrick Canyon Trail

SOUTH McKITTRICK CANYON

THE BOWL

Juniper Trail

Tejas Trail

Bush Mountain Trail

Blue Ridge Trail

PX FLAT

BROKEOFF MOUNTAINS

CUTOFF RIDGE

GUADALUPE

Frijole Ranch and History Exhibits

Corral

Smith Spring Trail

Frijole Trail

Foothills Trail

The Pinery

Bear Canyon Trail

Bowl Trail

Tejas Trail

PINE SPRING CANYON

Visitor Center
Park Headquarters

Pine Springs

Guadalupe Peak Trail

El Capitan Trail

Salt Basin Trail

El Capitan Trail

Salt Basin Overlook

Williams Ranch

M O U N T A I N S

GLOVER CANYON

Guadalupe Pass

GUADALUPE CANYON

Guadalupe Arroyo

DELAWARE MOUNTAIN

BRUSHY MESA

Gate

4wd vehicles only

Gate

62

NEW MEXICO
TEXAS

CROW FLATS

PATTERSON HILLS

SALT   BASIN

Legend

⬛	Ranger Station
▲	Campground
▲	Backcountry Campsites
	Dry Salt Lake

—— Paved Road
– – – 4wd Road
········· Hiking Trail
–·–·– Horse and Hiking Trail

0   3 Kilometers
0   3 Miles

GUADALUPE MOUNTAINS NATIONAL PARK

H.C. 60, Box 400
Salt Flat, TX 79847-9400
915-828-3251

The Guadalupe Mountains, part of one of the finest examples on Earth of an ancient marine fossil reef, were formed about 250 million years ago when a vast tropical ocean covered what is now west Texas and adjacent southern New Mexico. With elevations in the park extending from 3,660 feet to 8,749 feet above sea level, contrasts abound here, with high mountain forests giving way to arid desert, hot summer days turning to cool evenings, and seemingly barren landscapes that teem with life. Human history dates back 12,000 years, with the conflicts between the resident Apache Indians and pioneers, explorers, and the stage-coach traffic of the Butterfield Overland Mail Line adding to a colorful record of the 86,415-acre national park's past.

In 1959, Wallace F. Pratt donated 5,632 acres of the McKittrick Canyon area to the federal government, and the national park was established in 1972. Much of the park was designated a wilderness area in 1978.

OUTSTANDING FEATURES

Among the many outstanding features of the park are the following: **El Capitan**, a 2,000-foot-high peak jutting upward like the prow of an enormous ship at the southern end of the Guadalupe Mountains; **McKittrick Canyon**, a spectacular, sheer-walled, 2,000-foot-deep limestone canyon often called the most beautiful spot in Texas, sheltering a lush, ecologically rich riparian oasis along three miles of the only perennial stream in the park; **The Bowl**, a beautiful area of relict ice-age conifer forest; **Guadalupe Peak**, at 8,749 feet elevation, the highest point in the state of Texas; **Smith and Manzanita Springs**, two small oases that appear unexpectedly in the desert; and

Dog Canyon, a forested highland with spectacular views. Historic locations in the park include the ruins of **The Pinery**, the Pinery Station of the Butterfield Overland Mail Express dating from 1858; **Frijole Ranch**, an 1870s ranch house that is now the park's cultural history center; and the **Pratt Cabin**, in South McKittrick Canyon.

PRACTICAL INFORMATION

When to Go

The park is open year-round. Spring and fall are the best seasons to visit because the temperatures are mild, the days sunny, and the nights comfortable. Spring blossoms and late October-early November autumn foliage bring vivid colors to the scenery. Summer days are very hot and dry, but nights can be cool, especially at higher elevations.

How to Get There

By Car: From Carlsbad, drive southwest 55 miles on U.S. 62/180. From El Paso, drive east 110 miles on U.S. 62/180 to the short unpaved spur road to the park headquarters, main visitor center, and campground at Pine Springs.

By Air: Flights are available into the El Paso Airport (915-772-4271).

By Train: Amtrak (800-872-2745) has stops in El Paso.

By Bus: Greyhound Lines (800-231-2222) has stops closest to the park at Salt Flat, Texas.

Fees and Permits

There is no entrance fee. Free permits, required for backcountry camping, are available at Pine Springs Visitor Center or Dog Canyon Ranger Station.

Facilities

There are no lodgings, restaurants, or other facilities within the park's boundaries. Supplies are available in White's City, Carlsbad, Dell City, Van Horn, and El Paso.

57

▲ *El Capitan, Guadalupe Mountains National Park, Texas*

Handicapped Accessibility

Both visitor centers, a one-third mile trail from Pine Springs to the ruins of Butterfield Station, and one site and restrooms at the Pine Springs Campground are wheelchair accessible.

Medical Services

Limited first aid is available at Pine Springs and Dog Canyon. The closest hospital is in Carlsbad, New Mexico, 55 miles away.

Pets

Pets are allowed on leashes, but are prohibited in the backcountry, on trails, and in public buildings.

Safety and Regulations

For your safety and enjoyment and for the protection of the park, please follow these regulations and suggestions:

- Visitors should always carry one gallon of water per person per day and be alert for rattlesnakes and the spines of cacti.

- The National Park Service warns against climbing cliffs, which are dangerous because of unstable rocks and are unsafe even for technical climbs.

- Anticipate sudden changes in weather. Be prepared for thunderstorms in summer and violent winds in the spring and winter.

- All vehicles must stay on established roads.

- Firearms are strictly forbidden in the park.

- Remember that it is illegal to capture, hunt, feed, or otherwise disturb wildlife in the park, and trees and other plantlife are not to be cut or collected.

The National Park Service asks that visitors not litter the park. Remember the excellent slogan to "leave only footprints" as a guide to help protect this national park.

Visitor Centers, Museum, and Ranger Station

Pine Springs Visitor Center: open daily 8 a.m.-4:30 p.m. year-round; closed Christmas Day. Interpretive exhibits, publications, and maps.

McKittrick Canyon Visitor Center: open intermittently. Intepretive exhibits, maps, brochures.

Frijole Ranch: variable hours, depending on volunteer staff; usually open 8 a.m.-4:30 p.m; closed on Christmas Day. There is a history museum at this historic 1870s ranch house.

Dog Canyon Ranger Station: open daily 8 a.m.-4:30 p.m year-round; closed Christmas Day. Information.

ACTIVITIES

Options include hiking, backpacking, camping, horseback riding (no horse rentals), birdwatching, and wildflower identification.

Hiking Trails

The park provides over 80 miles of hiking trails, all of them well marked. The most popular is **McKittrick Canyon Trail**, part of which is a self-guided interpetive route at the northeast corner of the park. (A trail pamphlet is available at the McKittrick Canyon Visitor Center near the trailhead.) This exciting hike leads 2.3 miles up South McKittrick Canyon, along the delightful riparian habitat of the creek to the historic Pratt cabin. It is another mile along the creek to Grotto picnic area, from which the trail climbs steeply into the high country, connecting with other backcountry trails. From Frijole Ranch, the 2.3-mile **Manzanita and Smith Springs Loop Trail** provides good birdwatching opportunities at these Chihuahuan Desert oases, where maidenhair ferns, Texas madrones, and wildflowers thrive. From Pine Springs Campground, a number of trails lead up canyons and into the mountains, including the 9.5-mile loop hike through The Bowl, by way of **Bear Canyon, The Bowl,** and **Tejas trails**; the 4.6-mile **Guadalupe Peak Trail** that leads steeply up to the summit of the park's highest peak; and **El Capitan Trail** that winds around the base of the great rocky headland and leads ultimately to historic Williams Ranch on the west side of the mountains. Two park trailheads may be reached from the Lincoln National Forest, adjoining the

▲ *Storm clouds over gypsum dunes, Guadalupe Mountains National Park, Texas*

park in New Mexico: **Tejas Trail** in Upper Dog Canyon that leads through the high country and ultimately connects with Pine Springs Campground; and the **Permian Reef Geology Trail** that runs along the rim of Camp Wilderness Ridge, descends steeply into North McKittrick Canyon, and connects with McKittrick Canyon Trail.

OVERNIGHT STAYS

Lodging and Dining

No lodging or dining facilities are available in the park, but the communities of White's City, Carlsbad, Dell City, Van Horn, El Paso, and others offer many options.

Campgrounds

Pine Springs and Dog Canyon Campgrounds are open all year, and operate on a first-come, first-served basis with 14-day limits. Neither has showers or hookups. Fires are not permitted in the park; campstoves must be used for cooking. Pine Springs Campground, near the park's headquarters and main visitor center, has 38 RV/tent sites and two group sites that accommodate ten to 20 people. Dog Canyon Campground provides 13 RV/tent sites and one group site for six to 12 people. Reservations are recommended for group camping; call the park.

Backcountry Camping

Backcountry camping is allowed year-round at one of ten designated camping sites throughout much of the park, on a first-come, first-served basis. Free permits are required. Horses are not permitted overnight in the backcountry and can be stabled at Pine Springs and Dog Canyon corrals.

Mammals: elk, mule deer, black bear, mountain lion, bobcat, coyote, gray and kit foxes, javelina (peccary), badger, blacktail jack rabbit, desert and eastern cottontails, porcupine, raccoon, ringtail, several skunks, antelope and rock squirrels, spotted ground squirrel, and grayneck chipmunk.

Birds: wild turkey, scaled quail, red-tailed hawk, golden eagle, peregrine and prairie falcons, owls (flammulated, great horned, spotted, and screech), band-tailed pigeon, white-winged dove, roadrunner, hummingbirds (black-chinned, blue-throated, broad-tailed, and magnificent), acorn and ladder-backed woodpeckers, white-throated swift, violet-green and cliff swallows, raven, scrub and Steller's jays, mountain chickadee, plain titmouse, nuthatches (pygmy, red-breasted, and white-breasted), wrens (canyon, rock, cactus, and Bewick's), curve-billed thrasher, Townsend's solitaire, hermit thrush, western bluebird, warblers (black-throated gray, Grace's, orange-crowned, Wilson's, MacGillivray's, and yellow-rumped), Scott's oriole, hepatic and western tanagers, sparrows (black-chinned, black-throated, and rufous-crowned), canyon and rufous-sided towhees, pyrrhuloxia, and black-headed and blue grosbeaks.

Amphibians and Reptiles: Couch's spadefoot and red-spotted toads, lizards (crevice spiny, side-blotched, southern prairie, and tree), black-necked garter snake, kingsnake, coachwhip, and black-tailed, rock, and western diamondback rattlesnakes.

Trees, Shrubs, and Flowers: More than 1,000 species of trees and plants have been recorded in the park. The peak of autumn foliage color of the maples, walnuts, ashes, and other vegetation normally occurs in late October and early November. Trees and shrubs include pines (ponderosa, pinyon, and southwestern white), Douglas fir, alligator and one-seed junipers, Texas black walnut, oaks (Gambel's, chinkapin, gray, and wavyleaf), Knowlton hop hornbeam, quaking aspen, Texas madrone, Utah serviceberry, catclaw acacia, mesquite, Mexican buckeye, western soapberry, bigtooth maple, fragrant and velvet ashes, fendlerbush, creosotebush, ocotillo, lechuguilla and New Mexico agaves, sotol, and Faxon, Torrey, banana, and soaptree yuccas. There are more than 30 species of cacti, including Engelmann's prickly pear, cane cholla, green-flowered pitaya, and claretcup hedgehog. Among the multitude of wildflowers are Indian paintbrush, phlox, bladderpod, dwarf zinnia, Wright's vervain, evening primrose, globemallow, Chapline's columbine, penstemons (cardinal, Fendler's, southwestern, and James'), canyon sage, four o'clock, hairy resurrection plant, Texas and Lyre leaf greeneyes, biennial woolleywhite, birdbill and whitemouth dayflowers, goldenweed, goldeneyes, and prairie coneflower.

The areas surrounding Guadalupe Mountains National Park offer many exciting natural and cultural attractions that can be enjoyed as day trips or overnight excursions. Adjacent Lincoln National Forest and nearby Carlsbad Caverns are over the line in New Mexico; White Sands National Monument is to the northwest near Alamogordo, New Mexico; and Chamizal National Memorial, which honors the peaceful resolution of a border dispute between Mexico and the United States, is to the west in El Paso.

PETRIFIED FOREST NATIONAL PARK

▲ Pedestal logs in Blue Mesa

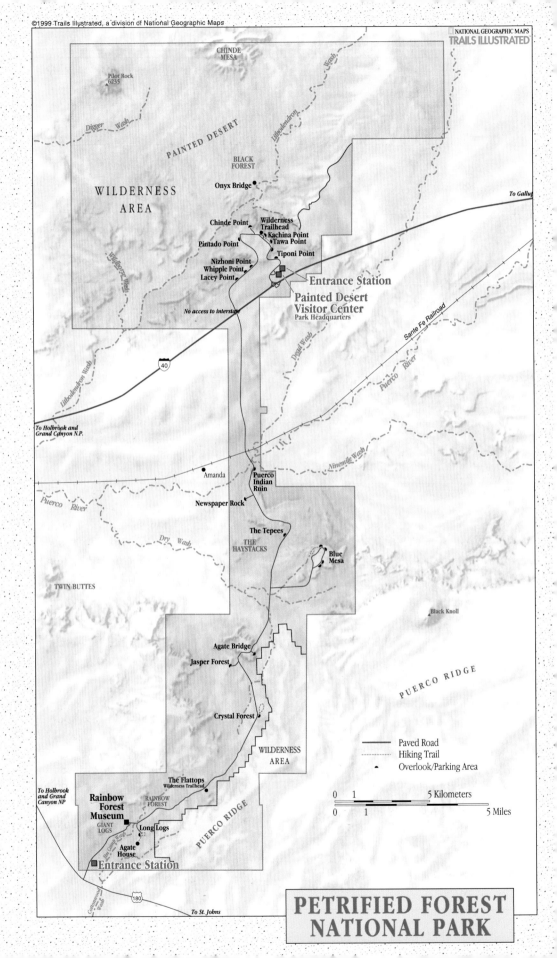

NATIONAL GEOGRAPHIC MAPS
TRAILS ILLUSTRATED

CHINDE MESA

Pilot Rock
6235

PAINTED DESERT

Digger Wash

Lithodendron Wash

BLACK FOREST

WILDERNESS AREA

Onyx Bridge

To Gallup

Chinde Point
Wilderness Trailhead
Kachina Point
Tawa Point
Pintado Point
Tiponi Point
Nizhoni Point
Whipple Point
Lacey Point

Wilderness Wash

Entrance Station
Painted Desert Visitor Center
Park Headquarters

No access to interstate

Sante Fe Railroad

Dead Wash

40

Puerco River

To Holbrook and
Grand Canyon N.P.

Ninemile Wash

Amanda
Puerco Indian Ruin

Newspaper Rock

Puerco River

Dry Wash

The Tepees

THE HAYSTACKS

Blue Mesa

TWIN BUTTES

Black Knoll

Agate Bridge
Jasper Forest

PUERCO RIDGE

Crystal Forest

WILDERNESS AREA

Paved Road
Hiking Trail
Overlook/Parking Area

The Flattops
Wilderness Trailhead

PUERCO RIDGE

0   1   5 Kilometers
0   1   5 Miles

To Holbrook
and Grand
Canyon NP

Rainbow Forest Museum

RAINBOW FOREST

GIANT LOGS
Long Logs
Agate House

Entrance Station

180

To St. Johns

PETRIFIED FOREST
NATIONAL PARK

Petrified Forest National Park

P.O. Box 2217
Petrified Forest National Park, AZ
86028
520-524-6228

In a corner of the Painted Desert in northeastern Arizona exists one of the world's largest concentrations of brilliantly colored petrified wood and fossilized animal remains. This land still reveals traces of what it once was during the upper Triassic Period of 225 million years ago, when stately conifer trees grew at the headwaters of streams that crossed a vast floodplain. Research has revealed that the park contains an incredible wealth of fossils of many ancient animals, including a ten-foot-long amphibian, a six-foot-long scaled fish, a 15-foot-long crocodile-like creature, a rhinoceros-like animal with tusks and a parrot-like head, and various kinds of primitive dinosaurs. Recent scientific discoveries suggest that this may be the best place anywhere in the world for early dinosaur fossils, making Petrified Forest a world-class paleontological national park.

The starkly beautiful desert landscape of this 93,532-acre park also contains important archaeological sites indicating human occupation dating back 10,000 years, expanses of high-desert shortgrass prairie, and the spectacularly colorful Painted Desert badlands. Proclaimed a national monument in 1906, the area was established as a national park in 1962. Some of the park was designated a wilderness area in 1970.

OUTSTANDING FEATURES

Among the many outstanding features of the park are the following, listed from north to south along the 28-mile park drive: **Tiponi, Kachina, Pintado,** and **Lacey points**, which provide panoramas of the reddish Painted Desert; **Puerco Indian Ruin**, the partially excavated remains of a one-story, 125-room prehistoric Anasazi pueblo that housed as many as 200 men, women, and children from around 1250 to 1380; **The Tepees**, bare cone-shaped mudstone formations in reddish and bluish colors caused by iron, manganese, and other minerals; **Blue Mesa**, an area reached by a three-mile spur road where pedestal logs abound through strange badlands layered in blue, purple, and cream colors; **Crystal Forest**, a major concentration of petrified logs that once held beautiful clear quartz and amethyst crystals; **The Flattops**, the massive remnants of a once-continuous layer of sandstone capping the area; **Long Logs**, the largest concentration of petrified wood in the park, with logs up to 170 feet long and colorful cross sections of fossil trees; and **Agate House**, a partially restored four-room Anasazi pueblo built partly of pieces of petrified wood.

PRACTICAL INFORMATION

When to Go

The park is open daily from 8 a.m. to 5 p.m, except Christmas Day and New Year's Day. Hours may be extended in summer. Summer begins hot with dry winds and progresses into the rainy season, which brings spectacular thunderstorms and half the year's total precipitation. Many species of wildflowers bloom in late summer, after the summer rains. Some of the best weather for this region is in the autumn. Winter brings periods of cold winds, along with some rain, relatively mild days, and occasional snow.

How to Get There

By Car: The Painted Desert (north) entrance to the park is off I-40 (the freeway slices through the northern end of the park), 25 miles east of Holbrook, Arizona, and 64 miles west of Gallup, New Mexico. From Holbrook, the Rainbow Forest (south) entrance is east 19 miles on U.S. Route 180.

By Air: The nearest airport is Flagstaff Pulliam Airport (520-556-1234).

By Train: Amtrak (800-872-7245) has stops in Gallup, New Mexico, and Winslow and Flagstaff, Arizona.

▲ *Puerco ruins, Anasazi village site, Petrified Forest National Park, Arizona*

By Bus: Greyhound Lines (800-231-2222) has stops in Holbrook.

Fees and Permits

Entrance fees are $10 per car for seven consecutive days or $5 per person on foot, bicycle, motorcycle, or bus. Free permits are required for backcountry camping.

Visitor Center and Museums

Painted Desert Visitor Center, just off I-40 near the northern end of the park: open daily all year. Interpretive exhibits, programs, and publications. Adjacent cafeteria and gift shop.

Painted Desert Inn Museum, on Kachina

Facilities

Available are a cafeteria, service station, gift shops, and picnic areas.

Handicapped Accessibility

Visitor centers, museum, and concessions are accessible. Call park headquarters for a detailed accessibility guide.

Medical Services

First aid is available in the park. The closest hospitals are in Winslow, 50 miles to the west, and Gallup, New Mexico, 64 miles to the east.

Pets

Pets are allowed on leashes, but not in public buildings or wilderness areas. Horseback riding is permitted, in groups of up to six riders; no grazing is allowed.

Safety and Regulations

For your safety and enjoyment and for the protection of the park, please follow these regulations and suggestions:

- It is recommended that visitors stay on trails and carry plenty of water.

- Do not climb on petrified logs.

- Remember that it is illegal to remove even the smallest piece of petrified wood or fossil. Removal of any petrified wood or any other natural, cultural, or historical object is a federal offense.

- The National Park Service warns visitors to avoid ground squirrels and other wild animals as they may carry bubonic plague.

Point near the northern end of the park: open only in summer. Historic pueblo-style building provides an interpretive center on Native American cultures of the Southwest.

Rainbow Forest Museum, at the southern end of the park: open daily all year, except Christmas and New Year's Day. Interpretive exhibits on petrified wood, geological history, and human history; concession gift shop.

ACTIVITIES

Options include hiking, ranger-led interpretive walks and talks, picnicking, backcountry camping (free permit required), and horseback riding (there are no rentals in the park).

Further information is available in the park's newspaper, *Petrified Forest National Park*.

Hiking Trails

Among the trails in the park are the quarter-mile **Painted Desert Wilderness Trail**, which starts on Kachina Point near the Painted Desert Inn interpretive center; the one-mile paved **Blue Mesa Trail**; the half-mile paved **Agate House Trail**; the half-mile loop **Long Logs Trail**; and behind the Rainbow Forest Museum, the half-mile **Giant Logs Trail**.

OVERNIGHT STAYS

Lodging

Lodging facilities are not available within the park. The communities such as Holbrook and Winslow, Arizona, and Gallup, New Mexico, offer many facilities.

Backcountry Camping

Camping in the backcountry is allowed all year throughout much of the park with a free permit available at visitor centers or the museum before 4 p.m

FLORA AND FAUNA (Partial Listings)

Mammals: mule deer, pronghorn, bobcat, coyote, badger, blacktail jack rabbit, desert cottontail, gray and kit foxes, whitetail prairie dog, porcupine, spotted and striped skunks, rock and whitetail antelope squirrels, spotted ground squirrel, and Ord kangaroo rat.

Birds: killdeer, red-tailed and Swainson's hawks, golden eagle, kestrel, prairie falcon, great horned and burrowing owls, roadrunner, black-chinned and broad-tailed hummingbirds, western and Cassin's kingbirds, Say's phoebe, horned lark, white-throated swift, swallows (violet-green, rough-winged, and cliff), raven, scrub jay, rock wren, mockingbird, western and mountain bluebirds, loggerhead shrike, western meadowlark, northern oriole, western tanager, sparrows (white-crowned, lark, black-throated, chipping, and vesper), rufous-sided and green-tailed towhees, and lesser goldfinch.

Amphibians and Reptiles: toads (western and Couch's spadefoot, Woodhouse's, and red-spotted), lizards (collared, side-blotched, and southern prairie), striped whipsnake, gopher snake, black-necked garter snake, and western rattlesnake.

Trees, Shrubs, Flowers, and Grasses: one-seed juniper (a few widely scattered), Fremont cottonwood and willow (along Rio Puerco Wash), cliffrose, rabbitbrush, sagebrush, four-winged saltbush, greasewood, ephedra, skunkbush, banana and narrowleaf yuccas, Whipple cholla, prickly pear, yellow mariposa lily, red penstemon, scarlet gilia, globemallow, Indian paintbrush, evening primrose, blazingstar, golden buckwheat, Engelmann aster, sunflowers, Indian ricegrass, alkali sacaton, dropseed, and sideoats, blue, hairy, Rothrock, six-weeks, mat, black, and needle grama grasses.

NEARBY POINTS OF INTEREST

The areas surrounding Petrified Forest National Park offer many other exciting natural and historical attractions that can be enjoyed as day trips or overnight excursions. Located within the northeast quadrant of Arizona are Walnut Canyon, Sunset Crater, Navajo, Canyon de Chelly, and Wupatki national monuments and Hubbell Trading Post National Historic Site. Just over the line in New Mexico are El Morro and El Malpais national monuments.

PETROGLYPH NATIONAL MONUMENT

▲ Rio Grande style petroglyphs

PETROGLYPH NATIONAL MONUMENT

Paradise

PIEDRAS MARCADAS CANYON

Boulevard

Pase

Calle Nortena

Taylor Ranch

Northern Geologic Window

BOCA NEGRA CANYON

Homestead

Golf Course

La C

BUTTE VOLCANO

BOND VOLCANO

Southern Geologic Window

Unser

Taylor Ranch

Montaño

Boulevard

Dellyne

448

Coors

VULCAN VOLCANO

Interim Visitor Center ■

Western Trail

BLACK VOLCANO

Arisco

Ladera

JA VOLCANO

St. Joseph

Ladera

Rio Grande

Paseo Del Vulcan

RINCONADA CANYON

MESA PRIETA

Ouray

96th Street

Unser

Ladera

40

do Albu

To Interstate 40

Boulevard

Paved Road
Unpaved Road

0   1 Kilometer
0   1 Mile

40

40

Petroglyph National Monument

**6001 Unser Boulevard, N.W.
Albuquerque, NM 87120
505-899-0205**

One of the Southwest's most extensive concentrations of rock art, carved into basalt boulders by prehistoric Indians and later Hispanics, lies along a 17-mile stretch of the West Mesa lava-flow escarpment across the Rio Grande from downtown Albuquerque. This 7,240-acre national monument protects more than 15,000 petroglyph images, a few of which may date as far back as 1000 B.C., while the majority date from around A.D. 1300 to 1650. Many of the latter petroglyphs portray masked and plumed ceremonial figures; the hump-backed, flute-playing fertility figure, Kokopelli; and images of such animals as deer, mountain lions, birds, lizards, and snakes. More than 60 shrines and other associated archaeological sites and five small cinder cones are also located within the monument.

As a result of a proposal by University of New Mexico students and other individuals, parts of the West Mesa area were established as state and municipal parks in the 1960s. In 1986, the whole petroglyph escarpment, called Las Imagines National Archeological District, was listed on the National Register of Historic Places. The national monument was established in 1990. It is jointly owned and managed by the National Park Service, the state of New Mexico, and the city of Albuquerque's Open Space Division.

NPCA worked cooperatively with Friends of the Albuquerque Petroglyphs and others in advocating establishment of the monument, and subsequently helped reach agreement with a local developer to ensure public access to the portion of the monument containing the highest concentration of petroglyphs. NPCA and Native American and historic preservation groups are presently struggling to defeat a proposal by the city of Albuquerque's highway department to construct a six-lane highway through the northern part of the monument.

This development would wipe out multitudes of irreplaceable petroglyphs and Native American religious sites.

ACTIVITIES

Options include self-guided and ranger-led tours. Further information is available in the park's newspaper, *Echoes from Petroglyph National Monument.*

PRACTICAL INFORMATION

When to Go

The monument is open daily year-round.

How to Get There

By Car: Exit I-40 onto Unser Boulevard and follow it north 2.5 miles to the visitor center.

By Air: Albuquerque International Airport (505-842-4366) serves most major airlines.

By Train: Amtrak (800-872-7245) has stops at Albuquerque Station.

By Bus: Greyhound Lines (800-231-2222) has stops at Albuquerque Transportation Center.

Fees and Permits

A $1 per vehicle parking fee is charged on weekdays and $2 on weekends and holidays.

Visitor Center

Petroglyph Visitor Center: open daily 8 a.m.-6 p.m in summer and 8 a.m.-5 p.m in winter; closed Thanksgiving, Christmas Day, and New Year's Day. Interpretive information, restrooms, and drinking water.

Facilities

Food and supplies are available throughout Albuquerque.

Handicapped Accessibility

The visitor center and parts of the Boca Negro Unit are accessible.

▲ *Image carved into basalt lava rock, Petroglyph National Monument, New Mexico*

Medical Services

Services are available in Albuquerque.

FLORA AND FAUNA (Partial Listings)

Mammals: pronghorn, coyote, gray and kit foxes, blacktail jackrabbit, desert cottontail, prairie dog, rock squirrel, antelope ground squirrel, and kangaroo rat.

Birds: Gambel's and scaled quail, red-tailed hawk, kestrel, great horned and burrowing owls, roadrunner, black-chinned hummingbird, Say's phoebe, horned lark, swallows including the violet-green, raven, rock and canyon wrens, loggerhead shrike, meadowlark, and black-throated and white-crowned sparrows.

Reptiles: whiptail and collared lizards, gopher and coachwhip snakes, and western rattlesnake.

Shrubs, Flowers, and Grasses: bird-of-paradise, broom dahlia, broom snakeweed, rabbitbrush, four-winged saltbush, winterfat, sand sagebrush, cholla and prickly pear cactus, globemallow, yellow puccoon, asters, sunflowers, and Indian ricegrass.

NEARBY POINTS OF INTEREST

Natural and cultural areas within a day's drive of the monument and Albuquerque include Salinas, Pecos, Bandelier, El Malpais, and El Morro national monuments; Coronado and Jemez state monuments; the Sandia Mountains unit of Cibola National Forest; Sevillita and Bosque del Apache national wildlife refuges; and numerous Pueblo Indian villages, such as Santo Domingo, San Ildefonso, Santa Clara, and Acoma.

SAGUARO NATIONAL PARK

▲ *Saguaro cactus*

Saguaro National Park

3693 S. Old Spanish Trail
Tucson, AZ 85730-5699
520-733-5153

The mighty saguaro cactus (pronounced sah-WAH-roh), growing to 40 feet or more and living perhaps 200 years, is a major attraction of this national park and the symbol of the ecologically rich Sonoran Desert of southern Arizona. This scenic, two-unit park of 91,452 acres protects a magnificent diversity of scenic flora and fauna. Elevations in the park range from about 2,500 to 8,666 feet above sea level—from low desert to the jagged summits of the Tucson Mountains, just west of the city of Tucson, and to rich pine and fir forests in the Rincon Mountains, just east of Tucson.

The area was proclaimed a national monument in 1933, when it was transferred from the U.S. Forest Service. Much of the area was designated wilderness in 1976, and it was established as a national park in 1994. Recently, NPCA initiated negotiations with landowners and others that succeeded in a congressionally approved 3,500-acre expansion of the park's Rincon Mountain District and has worked with local park advocates to gain congressional approval to expand the Tucson Mountain District and redesignated the entire area's status from a national monument to a national park.

OUTSTANDING FEATURES

Among the outstanding features of the park are the saguaro and more than 50 other species of cacti and an abundance of other plantlife and wildlife.

PRACTICAL INFORMATION

When to Go

The park is open year-round (Rincon Mountain District is open only in daylight hours). Late autumn, winter, and early spring are normally mild, with sunshine nearly every day and occasional winter rains. Late spring, early summer, and early autumn are normally clear and hot, with extremely low humidity and temperatures often topping 100 degrees F. July, August, and early September are the so-called "monsoon" season, bringing dramatic thunderstorms, heavy downpours, higher humidity, and slightly lower temperatures, but at least some sunshine virtually every day.

How to Get There

By Car: To reach the Rincon Mountain District, follow Old Spanish Trail from Broadway Blvd., or Harrison or Houghton roads at the eastern edge of Tucson to the entrance. To reach the Tucson Mountain District, follow Speedway Blvd., west at the west edge of Tucson, crossing over Gates Pass in Tucson Mountain Park, and proceeding northwest on Kinney Road two miles beyond the Arizona-Sonora Desert Museum.

By Air: Tucson International Airport (520-573-8000) is served by a number of major airlines.

By Train: Amtrak (800-872-7245) has stops in Tucson.

By Bus: Greyhound Lines (800-231-2222) has stops in Tucson. Arizona Shuttle Service (800-888-2749) runs express service between Phoenix's Sky Harbor Airport and Tucson.

Fees and Permits

Entrance fees are $4 per vehicle and $2 per person, both valid for seven consecutive days in the Rincon Mountain District. Free permits for backcountry camping in the Rincon Mountain Wilderness are required and are available at the visitor center. No entrance fee is charged at the Tucson Mountain District.

Visitor Centers

Red Hills Information Center, in the Tucson Mountain District (west). Interpretive exhibits, programs, publications, trail and drive guides, and maps.

Rincon Visitor Center, in the Rincon Mountain District (east). Interpretive exhibits, programs, publications, trail and drive guides, and maps.

SAGUARO WEST

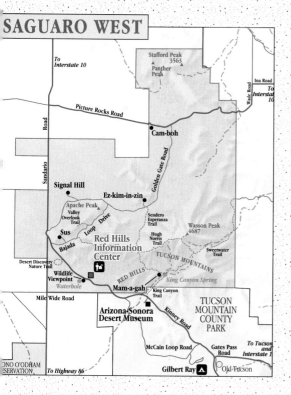

SAGUARO NATIONAL PARK

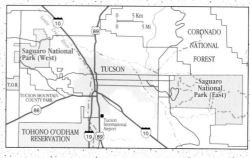

To Interstate 10
Picture Rocks Road
Stafford Peak 3563
Panther Peak
Cam-boh
Ina Road
To Interstate 10
Wade Road
Golden Gate Road
Sandario Road
Signal Hill
Ez-kim-in-zin
Apache Peak
Valley Overlook Trail
Loop Drive
Sendero Esperanza Trail
Wasson Peak 4687
Sus
Bajada
Hugh Norris Trail
Red Hills Information Center
TUCSON MOUNTAINS
Sweetwater Trail
Desert Discovery Nature Trail
Wildlife Viewpoint
RED HILLS
King Canyon Spring
Waterhole
Mam-a-gah
King Canyon Trail
Mile Wide Road
Arizona-Sonora Desert Museum
Kinney Road
TUCSON MOUNTAIN COUNTY PARK
ONO O'ODHAM SERVATION
To Highway 86
McCain Loop Road
Gates Pass Road
To Tucson and Interstate 1
Gilbert Ray
Old Tucson

CORONADO NATIONAL FOREST
Saguaro National Park (West)
TUCSON
Saguaro National Park (East)
T.O.R.
Tucson Mountain County Park
86
TOHONO O'ODHAM RESERVATION
Tucson International Airport
19 89
10
0   5 Km
0   5 Mi

Legend

— Paved Road	Ranger Station	0 — 3 Kilometers
— Unpaved Road	Campground	0 — 3 Miles
---- Hiking Trail	Backcountry Campsite	

SAGUARO EAST

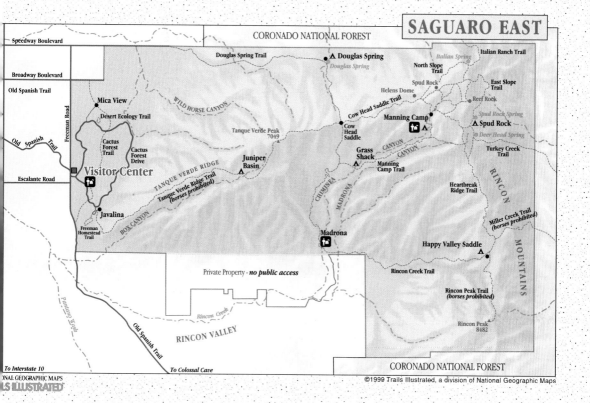

Speedway Boulevard
CORONADO NATIONAL FOREST
Broadway Boulevard
Old Spanish Trail
Douglas Spring Trail
Douglas Spring
Italian Spring
Italian Ranch Trail
North Slope Trail
Spud Rock
East Slope Trail
Helens Dome
Reef Rock
Mica View
Desert Ecology Trail
WILD HORSE CANYON
Cow Head Saddle Trail
Manning Camp
Spud Rock
Spud Rock Spring
Old Spanish Trail
Freeman Road
Cactus Forest Trail
Cactus Forest Drive
Tanque Verde Peak 7049
Cow Head Saddle
Deer Head Spring
Visitor Center
Grass Shack
Turkey Creek Trail
Escalante Road
TANQUE VERDE RIDGE
Juniper Basin
Manning Camp Trail
RINCON
Tanque Verde Ridge Trail (horses prohibited)
CHIMINEA CANYON
MADRONA CANYON
Heartbreak Ridge Trail
Javalina
BOX CANYON
Freeman Homestead Trail
Madrona
Miller Creek Trail (horses prohibited)
MOUNTAINS
Happy Valley Saddle
Private Property - no public access
Rincon Creek Trail
Panting Wash
Rincon Creek
Rincon Peak Trail (horses prohibited)
Old Spanish Trail
RINCON VALLEY
Rincon Peak 8482
To Interstate 10
To Colossal Cave
CORONADO NATIONAL FOREST

Handicapped Accessibility

Visitor centers, restrooms, and several trails are wheelchair accessible. Modified latrines are available at some picnic areas, and a captioned audiovisual program for the hearing-impaired is also available.

Medical Services

First aid is available in both districts. A number of major hospitals are available in Tucson.

Pets

Pets are allowed on leashes, but not in the backcountry, on trails, or in public buildings.

Safety and Regulations

For your safety and enjoyment and for the protection of the park, please follow these regulations and suggestions:

- Especially on hikes in hot, dry weather, carry at least one gallon of water per person per day. Pace yourself in extreme heat, and drink water even if you don't feel thirsty. Because perspiration evaporates instantly in the dry desert air, you can easily become dehydrated.

- Be alert for rattlesnakes, cacti, and other thorny plants. Gila monsters, while appearing to be sluggish lizards, inflict a tenacious and toxic bite.

- Avoid exposed areas and washes during thunderstorms, as lightning and flash flooding pose risks.

- Motor vehicles must remain on established roads.

- Firearms are strictly forbidden.

- Remember that it is illegal to feed, pet, hunt, capture, or otherwise disturb wildlife.

The National Park Service asks that visitors not litter the park. Remember the excellent slogan to "leave only footprints" as a guide to help protect this national park.

ACTIVITIES

Options include hiking, birdwatching, spring desert wildflower identification, picnicking, backcountry camping (Rincon Mountain District only), horseback riding, bicycling, and ranger-led interpretive walks.

Scenic Drives

The eight-mile Cactus Forest Drive loops through the Rincon Mountain District. The six-mile, unpaved Bajada Loop Drive winds through the Tucson Mountain District.

Hiking Trails

In the Rincon Mountain District: More than 120 miles of trails include the quarter-mile, self-guided interpretive **Desert Ecology Trail; Cactus Forest Trail**, part of which is available for mountain biking; the scenic **Tanque Verde Ridge Trail**, climbing from Javelina Picnic Area to 7,049-foot Tanque Verde Peak; **Turkey Creek Trail**, which climbs steeply up the east side of the Rincons; numerous trails in the vicinity of 8,666-foot Mica Peak and Manning Camp; and **Rincon Peak Trail**, which climbs to the summit of 8,482-foot Rincon Peak. All except Tanque Verde Ridge, Miller Creek, and Rincon Peak trails are open to horseback riding.

In the Tucson Mountain District: More than 40 miles of trails include the short, paved, interpretive **Cactus Garden Trail** at the information center; the half-mile **Discovery Nature Trail** that loops from the information center through a nearby stretch of desert bajada terrain; the 1.5-mile round-trip **Valley Overlook Trail**, amid beautiful expanses of saguaros, providing outstanding mountain and valley panoramas; and longer trails offering more challenging treks into the mountains. All trails are open to horseback riding.

OVERNIGHT STAYS

Lodging and Dining

While no lodging or dining facilities are located within the park, many are available in the adjacent city of Tucson.

Campgrounds

No campgrounds are located within the national park, although there is one in Pima

County's Tucson Mountain Park and others are in Coronado National Forest. Backcountry camping is allowed year-round at designated sites within the Rincon Mountain District, for which a free permit is required. Those sites have a seven-day limit and are either hike-in or horseback ride-in. Douglas Springs, Grass Shacks, Happy Valley, Juniper Basin, and Spud Rock campgrounds have three sites each; Manning Camp has six. Fires are permitted only at designated grates or campstoves. There are two picnic areas in the Rincon Mountain district and five picnic areas in the Tucson Mountain district, including one reached by trail.

FLORA AND FAUNA (Partial Listings)

Mammals: black bear, mule and whitetail deer, mountain lion, bobcat, gray and kit foxes, badger, porcupine, raccoon, coati, ringtail, blacktail jackrabbit, desert cottontail, skunks (spotted, striped, hooded, and hognose), squirrels (Abert's, Arizona gray, and rock), roundtail and Yuma antelope ground squirrels, cliff chipmink, kangaroo rats, and woodrats.

Birds: hawks (red-tailed, zone-tailed, Harris', and black), golden eagle, prairie and peregrine falcons, quail (scaled, Gambel's, and Harlequin), wild turkeys, band-tailed pigeons, doves (white-winged, mourning, and Inca), roadrunner, owls (screech, whiskered, flammulated, great horned, elf, and spotted), white-throated swift, hummingbirds (black-chinned, Costa's, Anna's, broad-tailed, rufous, magnificent or Rivoli's, blue-throated, and broad-billed), gilded flicker, woodpeckers (Gila, acorn, ladder-backed, and Strickland's), ash-throated and vermilion flycatchers, Say's phoebe, violet-green and cliff swallows, purple martin, jays (Steller's, scrub, and Mexican), raven, Clark's nutcracker, mountain chickadee, bridled titmouse, verdin, bushtit, nuthatches (white-breasted, red-breasted, and pygmy), wrens (cactus, rock, canyon, Bewick's, and house), mockingbird, thrashers (curve-billed, Bendire's, and crissal), hermit thrush, western and mountain bluebirds, Townsend's solitaire, black-tailed and blue-gray gnatcatchers,

ruby-crowned kinglet, phainopepla, numerous species of warblers including Wilson's, orange-crowned, Nashville, Virginia's, Lucy's, olive, yellow-rumped, black-throated gray, Townsend's, hermit, Grace's, MacGillivray's, red-faced, yellowthroat, painted redstart, and yellow-breasted chat, orioles (Bullock's, hooded, and Scott's), western and hepatic tanagers, cardinal, pyrrhuloxia, black-headed grosbeak, evening grosbeak, Cassin's finch, lesser goldfinch, red crossbill, towhees (green-tailed, rufous-sided, and canyon), numerous sparrows including rufous-crowned, black-throated, black-chinned, and white-crowned, and dark-eyed and gray-headed juncoes.

Amphibians and Reptiles: Arizona coral snake, canyon treefrog, leopard frog, red-spotted and Colorado River toads, Couch's and western spadefoot toads, desert tortoise, Gila monster and numerous lizards including collared, zebra-tailed, side-blotched, desert spiny, and several species of horned, Arizona coral snake, coachwhip, gopher snake, and western diamondback, black-tailed, tiger, and western rattlesnakes.

Trees, Shrubs, and Flowers: pines (southwestern white, Mexican pinyon, ponderosa, and Chihuahua), Douglas fir, white fir, Arizona cypress, alligator and one-seed junipers, Arizona sycamore, netleaf hackberry, oaks (Gambel's, Mexican blue, Arizona white, Emory, turbinella, Palmer, netleaf, Toumey, and silverleaf), quaking aspen, catclaw acacia, mesquite, yellow and blue paloverdes, New Mexico locust, desert ironwood, mountain mahogany, pointleaf manzanita, creosotebush, brittlebush, jojoba, indigobush (Dalea), fairy-duster, ocotillo, desert marigold, Parry's penstemon, globemallow, lupine, scalloped phacelia, bluedicks, white tackstem, fiddleneck, agaves, sotol, and yuccas. The numerous species of cacti include saguaro, fishhook barrel, chollas (chainfruit, teddy bear, cane, pencil, buckthorn, Christmas, and staghorn), cream and fishhook pincushions, hedgehogs (clatecup, Arizona rainbow, and Fendler), night-blooming cereus, and Engelmann, purple, purple-fruited, smooth, and pancake prickly pears.

▲ *Desert storm, Saguaro National Park, Arizona*

NEARBY POINTS OF INTEREST

Coronado National Forest, part of which surrounds the park's Rincon Mountain District, provides campgrounds, hiking trails, and picnic areas. An outstanding drive is the Mt. Lemmon Highway that winds into the conifer forests, high in the rugged Santa Catalina Mountains of Coronado National Forest, to the north of Tucson. Pima County's 17,000-acre Tucson Mountain Park (520-883-4200) adjoining the national park's Tucson Mountain District protects a beautiful area of saguaro-studded desert and jagged peaks and offers hiking and horse trails, picnic areas, and a campground. Within the county park is the famous

Arizona Sonora Desert Museum (520-883-2702) presenting outstanding exhibits of more than 200 species of desert wildlife, including hummingbirds, and several hundred kinds of desert plantlife. Also within a day's drive of the national park are Organ Pipe Cactus National Monument (protecting another outstanding area of Sonoran Desert), Chiricahua National Monument, Ft. Bowie National Historic Site, Coronado National Memorial, Tumacacori National Historical Park, Catalina State Park, Buenos Aires National Wildlife Refuge, Aravaipa Canyon Wilderness, the U.S. Bureau of Land Management's San Pedro Riparian National Conservation Area, and The Nature Conservancy's Patagonia-Sonoita Creek Preserve (520-622-3861).

WALNUT CANYON NATIONAL MONUMENT

▲ Cliff dwellings

Walnut Canyon National Monument

Walnut Canyon Road
Flagstaff, AZ 86004-9705
520-526-1157

Sometime before A.D. 600, groups of prehistoric Indians now referred to as the Sinagua (Spanish for "without water") began moving into the vicinity of the San Francisco Peaks in northern Arizona. As scattered family groups, they lived off the land by hunting, gathering, and small-scale farming, but gradually they began coming together in small settlements. Between A.D. 1125 and the early 1200s, the winding course of 400-foot-deep Walnut Canyon became the focus of an important community. Along narrow, sheltering ledges in the canyon's sheer limestone cliffs, roughly 150 feet above the canyon bottom, the Indians built dwellings of limestone blocks set in mortar. More than 80 of these structures, with more than 300 small rooms lined up end-to-end, were neatly nestled into ledges sheltered by cliff overhangs. The ruins of these cliff dwellings are still visible today, and the monument also protects a number of mesa-top Indian ruins.

The area was proclaimed a national monument in 1915 and was transferred from the U.S. Forest Service in 1933. More recently, at NPCA's instigation and with help from the local Friends of Walnut Canyon, Congress approved expanding the national monument to protect additional important Indian ruin sites in the canyon. As a result, the monument now encompasses 3,541 acres.

OUTSTANDING FEATURES

Among the many outstanding features of the park are the Sinagua Indian cliff dwellings dating from the 12th century, a scenic canyon, and varied flora and fauna.

PRACTICAL INFORMATION

When to Go

The monument is open daily 7 a.m.-6 p.m from Memorial Day to Labor Day and 8 a.m.-5 p.m. the rest of the year. Closed Christmas Day.

How to Get There

By Car: From Flagstaff, drive east 7.5 miles on I-40 and then south three miles on the Walnut Canyon Road to the visitor center.

By Air: Flagstaff Pulliam Airport (520-556-1234) serves the area.

By Train: Amtrak (800-872-7245) has stops in Flagstaff.

By Bus: Greyhound Lines (800-231-2222) has stops in Flagstaff.

Fees and Permits

The entrance fee is $3 per person.

Visitor Center

Walnut Canyon Visitor Center, located at the heads of Island and Rim trails. Interpretive information.

Facilities

A picnic area is available in the monument. Lodgings and meals are available in Flagstaff.

Handicapped Accessibility

The visitor center, the Rim Trail, and restrooms are accessible.

Medical Services

Emergency first aid is available in the park. The closest hospital is in Flagstaff, ten miles away.

Pets

Pets are allowed on leashes but not in the visitor center or on the Island Trail.

Safety and Regulations

For your safety and enjoyment and for the protection of the park, please follow these regulations and suggestions:

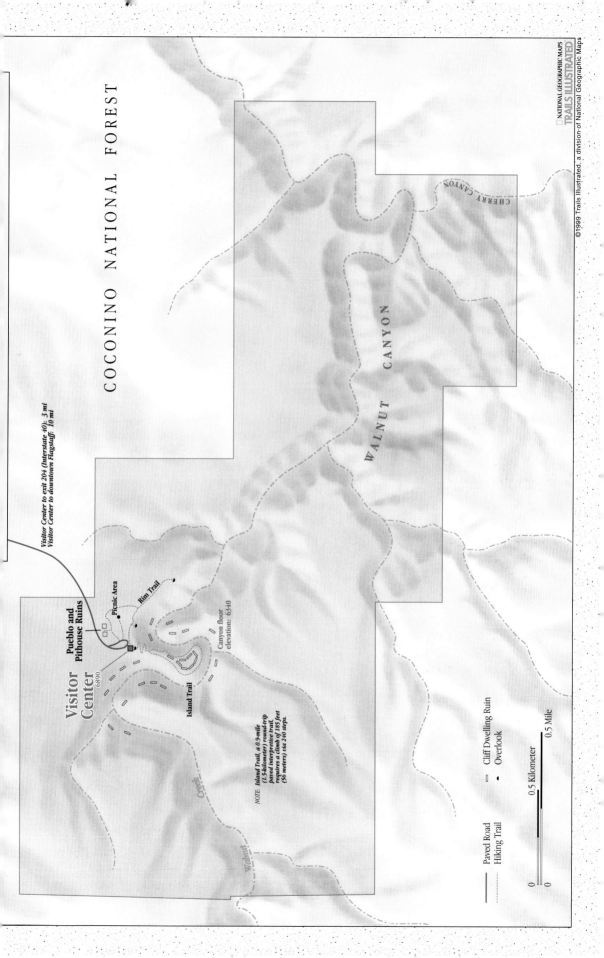

COCONINO NATIONAL FOREST

Visitor Center to exit 204 (Interstate 40): 3 mi
Visitor Center to downtown Flagstaff: 10 mi

CHERRY CANYON

WALNUT CANYON

Visitor
Center
6890

Pueblo and
Pithouse Ruins

Picnic Area

Rim Trail

Canyon floor
elevation: 6340

Island Trail

Creek

Walnut

NOTE: Island Trail, a 0.9-mile
(1.5-kilometer) round-trip
paved interpretive trail,
requires a climb of 185 feet
(56 meters) via 240 steps.

☐ Cliff Dwelling Ruin
• Overlook

——— Paved Road
········· Hiking Trail

0.5 Kilometer

0.5 Mile

0

0

- Because of the normally high fire danger, no open fires are permitted. Visitors who smoke or use portable stoves are urged to be extremely careful.
- All vehicles must remain on established roads, and hikers are required to stay on designated trails.

ACTIVITIES

Options include a self-guided interpretive walk to view cliff-dwelling ruins and ranger-led interpretive walks in summer. Further information is available in the park's newspaper, *Ancient Times*.

Hiking Trails

The nearly one-mile-long **Island Trail** descends 185 feet into Walnut Canyon and loops around a sharp bend in the canyon, providing opportunities to closely view some of the cliff-dwelling ruins and the varied flora and fauna. A pamphlet for this self-guided trail is available at the visitor center. (Note: With the elevation at about 6,800 feet above sea level, visitors are cautioned to carefully pace themselves descending and climbing back up this trail's several flights of steps.) In addition, the **Rim Trail** is a level walk that provides impressive views of the canyon.

FLORA AND FAUNA (Partial Listings)

Mammals: elk, mule deer, pronghorn, black bear, mountain lion, bobcat, coyote, gray fox, javelina (peccary), cottontail, porcupine, raccoon, ringtail, spotted and striped skunks, Abert and rock squirrels, golden-mantled ground squirrel, and cliff chipmunk.

Birds: wild turkey, red-tailed and Cooper's hawks, golden eagle, peregrine falcon, great horned and spotted owls, black-chinned hummingbird, flicker, white-throated swift, violet-green swallow, raven, Steller's and pinyon jays, mountain chickadee, plain titmouse, bushtit, pygmy and white-breasted nuthatches, rock and canyon wrens, hermit thrush, warblers (black-throated gray, Grace's, Virginia's, yellow-rumped, and red-faced), northern oriole, hepatic and western tanagers, rufous-sided towhee, dark-eyed and gray-headed juncoes, black-headed grosbeak, and red crossbill.

Trees, Shrubs, and Flowers: ponderosa and pinyon pines, junipers (Utah, Rocky Mountain, alligator, and one-seed), Douglas fir, Arizona black walnut (for which the canyon is named), Gambel's oak, narrowleaf cottonwood, quaking aspen, New Mexico locust, boxelder, mountain mahogany, Utah serviceberry, cliffrose, ephedra, agave, wax currant, blue elder, wild grape, Oregon grape, common hoptree, lemonade sumac, yuccas (datil, banana, and narrowleaf), penstemon, Indian paintbrush, several species of cacti, lupine, globemallow, and aster.

NEARBY POINTS OF INTEREST

Within a day's drive of Walnut Canyon are Grand Canyon and Petrified Forest national parks; Sunset Crater, Wupatki, Montezuma Castle, and Tuzigoot national monuments; and Coconino National Forest, which surrounds the monument.

OTHER NATIONAL PARK UNITS IN THE SOUTHWEST REGION

▲ *The Sonoran Desert, Organ Pipe Cactus National Monument, Arizona*

Other National Park Units in the Southwest Region

ARIZONA

Casa Grande Ruins National Monument

1100 Ruins Drive
Coolidge, AZ 85228
520-723-3172

This 472-acre national monument in south-central Arizona protects the ruins of the largest known structure of the Hohokam people, who farmed the valleys of the Gila and Salt rivers in the Sonoran Desert for about 1,500 years. Casa Grande (as early Spanish explorers called this "Great House") was built around A.D. 1350 and is four stories high and 60 feet long. Its adobe walls face the four cardinal points of the compass and have openings that align with the sun and moon at specific times of day. This alignment suggests that the Hohokam (a Pima Indian word for "those who have gone") knew the land well and had identified the best times of year for planting, irrigating, harvesting, and ceremonial celebrations.

Interpretive exhibits, tours of the ruins, and a picnic area are provided. To reach the monument from Phoenix, drive south on I-10, take the Coolidge exit (#185), and proceed east 14 miles on State Route 387 and then east six miles on State Route 87. From Tucson, take the Coolidge exit (#211) from I-10, and drive north 20 miles through the town of Coolidge to the monument.

Chiricahua National Monument

Dos Cabezas Route, Box 6500
Willcox, AZ 85643
520-824-3560 or 9737

This scenic, 11,984-acre national monument in the Chiricahua Mountains of southeast Arizona consists of a vast array of weather-sculpted rock spires, columns, and massive balanced rocks. It was called the Land of the Standing-Up Rocks by the Chiricahua Apaches who once lived in these mountains, and later the Wonderland of Rocks by early pioneers. In the Heart of Rocks, hundreds of these towering formations are clustered together on the mountainsides and canyon slopes.

The monument road winds up Bonita Canyon and provides a grand panorama at Massai Point. Many miles of hiking trails loop through these towering formations and descend into forested canyons shaded by such trees as Arizona cypress, Douglas fir, alligator juniper, and madrone, along with Gambel, Toumey, Emory, Arizona white, netleaf, and silverleaf oaks and ponderosa, Apache, Mexican pinyon, and Chihuahua pines. Close to 700 species of flowering plants and ferns have been identified in the monument. Among the great variety of wildlife are coati, ringtail, javelina (peccaries), Apache fox squirrel, at least eight species of hummingbirds, bridled titmouse, gray-breasted jay, painted redstart, and three kinds of quail.

The site offers interpretive exhibits, a campground, and guided tours of the historic Faraway Ranch house. To reach the monument, drive southeast on I-10 from Willcox, Arizona, just over 30 miles on State Route 186 and then east several miles on State Route 181.

Coronado National Memorial

4101 E. Montezuma Canyon Road
Hereford, AZ 85615
520-366-5515

The first major European exploration of the American Southwest is commemorated by this national memorial in southeast Arizona. The scenic, 4,750-acre area extends along the U.S.-Mexican border at the southern end of the Huachuca Mountains within sight of the San Pedro River Valley to the east. Some historians believe that it was northward down this broad valley that the huge Spanish expedition of 1540-1542, led by Francisco Vasquez de Coronado, first entered what is now the United States in search of the fabled Seven Cities of Cibola.

The memorial's beautiful woodlands include ten species of oaks native to southeastern Arizona, along with such other trees as alligator juniper, Arizona madrone, and Arizona sycamore. Wildlife include coatis, ringtails, javelinas (peccaries), and more than

160 species of birds, including a dozen varieties of hummingbirds. Among the six miles of trails winding through the memorial, one leads hikers to the 6,864-foot summit of Coronado Peak. The visitor center features an interpretive video and exhibits, and a small picnic area is nearby. While camping is not allowed in the memorial, facilities are available in the adjacent national forest.

To reach the monument from I-10, just west of Benson, Arizona, drive south 29 miles to Sierra Vista on State Route 90, then south about 15 miles on State Route 92 and right onto Coronado Memorial Road.

Fort Bowie National Historic Site

P.O. Box 158
Bowie, AZ 85605
520-847-2500
This 1,000-acre site between the Chiricahua and Dos Cabezas mountains in southeast Arizona protects the ruins of Fort Bowie, a strategically placed military post established following the 1862 Battle of Apache Pass between 96 Union troops and more than 100 Chiricahua Apaches. A subsequent series of periodic clashes between U.S. soldiers and the Indians finally ended in 1886 with the defeat of Geronimo's band of Chiricahuas, after which Anglo-American settlement spread on throughout the region. The site also includes a Butterfield Overland Mail station, built in the late 1850s adjacent to a key source of water in Apache Pass.

A mile-and-a-half-long trail leads visitors to the ruins of the fort, and a trail from there follows a three-mile stretch of the old Butterfield stage road. A picnic area is provided, but camping is not permitted. To reach the site from I-10 at Willcox, Arizona, drive southeast 22 miles on State Route 186, turn left on Apache Pass Road, and proceed about nine miles to the trailhead.

Glen Canyon National Recreation Area

P.O. Box 1507
Page, AZ 86040-1507
520-608-6404
The 1.2-million-acre Glen Canyon National Recreation Area in northeast Arizona and southeast Utah provides a dramatic example of an inspiring natural setting that has been changed by an ambitious human enterprise. Initially, only earth forces shaped this grand topography that now appears as water- and wind-sculpted buttes, mesas, and sheer-walled canyons by the Colorado River. Prehistoric human inhabitants next occupied the area and left scattered evidence of their culture, and in 1963 the scene was profoundly changed when the Bureau of Reclamation built the Glen Canyon Dam, creating a reservoir behind it.

Now, houseboating, boat camping, water sports, and fishing are dominant activities on the 200-mile-long reservoir, named Lake Powell for 19th century scientist-explorer John Wesley Powell, while the rugged canyon and mesa country surrounding the lake offer an abundance of hiking opportunities. Not only are camping and picnicking facilities provided at a number of locations in the recreation area, but lodging, meals, and marinas are available at Wahweap, Bullfrog, Halls Crossing, and Hite. Interpretive information is offered at visitor centers; interpretive programs are provided at Wahweap during the summer months.

There are three ways to reach the site: on U.S. Route 89, near Page, Arizona; on Utah State Route 276, with a ferry connection across the lake between Bullfrog and Halls Crossing, Utah; and on Utah State Route 95 with a short spur road to Hite, Utah.

Hohokam Pima National Monument

c/o Casa Grande Ruins National
Monument
1100 Ruins Dr.
Coolidge, AZ 85228
520-723-3172
The monument, which is not currently open to the public, protects the Snaketown archaeological site, containing the remains of a large Hohokam Indian village occupied between A.D. 300 and 1100.

Hubbell Trading Post National Historic Site

P.O. Box 150
Ganado, AZ 86505
520-755-3475
John Lorenzo Hubbell (1853-1930), who was

considered the dean of traders to the Navajo Indians, built Hubbell Trading Post in 1883 on the Navajo Reservation in northeast Arizona. He was not only the Navajo's merchant, but also their trusted teacher who translated and wrote letters, negotiated disputes, interpreted governmental policies, and even cared for the sick. The trading post, illustrating the influence of reservation traders on the Indians' way of life, continues today largely as in the past—offering for sale such merchandise as groceries, hand-woven Navajo rugs, and Navajo, Zuni, and Hopi jewelry.

The site provides interpretive exhibits, silversmithing and weaving demonstrations, guided tours of the historic Hubbell family home, and a picnic area. Among access routes to the site are the following. From the Chambers, Arizona, exit at I-40, drive north 37 miles on U.S. Route 191 to Ganado, and then west about a half-mile on Route 191/State Route 264. Or from U.S. Route 160 at Tuba City, Arizona, drive east 125 miles on State Route 264. Or from Chinle, Arizona, near Canyon de Chelly National Monument, drive south 30 miles on U.S. Route 191 and east five miles on Route 191/State Route 264.

Juan Bautista de Anza National Historic Trail

National Park Service
600 Harrison Street, Suite 600
San Francisco, CA 94123
415-744-3975

This trail traces the route of a six-month Spanish expedition by 30 families and a dozen soldiers under the leadership of Col. Juan Bautista de Anza, who in 1776 sought to establish an overland route from central Mexico to the Golden Gate in California. This national historic trail extends 1,200 miles from Tubac, Arizona, through the desert of southwestern Arizona and southeastern California along the coast to San Francisco. Most of the trail is currently in the planning stage. Several short segments are open to the public, including a 4.5-mile stretch connecting Tumacacori National Historical Park and Tubac Presidio State Historical Park in Arizona.

Montezuma Castle National Monument

P.O. Box 219
Camp Verde, AZ 86322
520-634-5564

The Sinagua Indians inhabited the foothills and plateau beyond the Verde Valley in central Arizona until about A.D. 1125, when they moved into the warmer valley and began constructing large pueblos (villages) such as Montezuma Castle. The castle is ironically neither a castle nor a site with any connection to Montezuma or the Aztecs of Mexico. Rather, it is a five-story, 20-room stone structure built in a shallow cave 100 feet above the base of the cliff. Being 90 percent intact, it is one of the best-preserved cliff dwellings in the United States. The ruins of another pueblo structure lie at the cliff base nearby. Eleven miles from this main unit of the 857-acre national monument is Montezuma Well—a cliff-encircled, spring-fed pond that is 470 feet across. Above one side of the pond are the ruins of several small storage structures nestled into narrow cavities of the cliff. Beaver Creek flows through both units of the monument and is shaded by beautiful Arizona sycamore trees. Interpretive exhibits are provided at the visitor center, and picnic areas are available at both units.

Access from Phoenix is north 76 miles on I-17 to the Montezuma Castle exit, then just over two miles to the entrance. From the I-17/I-40 junction at Flagstaff, drive south 49 miles on I-17 to the Montezuma Castle exit.

Navajo National Monument

H.C. 71, Box 3
Tonalea, AZ 86044-9704
520-672-2366

This 360-acre national monument consists of three units, each of which protects the ruins of one of the largest prehistoric cave villages in Arizona. The Anasazi people ("enemy ancestors") of the Kayenta area, in this northern part of what is now the Navajo Reservation, grew crops of maize, beans, and squash in the bottom of sheer-walled, red sandstone canyons. The village in a large alcove in the south-facing cliff of 700-foot-deep Betatakin ("ledge house") Canyon was first developed around A.D.

1267. Within a decade, the village had grown to more than 100 rooms and ultimately housed around 125 men, women, and children. By the end of that century, Betatakin was abandoned. A few miles away, two other cave villages were similarly established and abandoned: one in Keet Seel ("broken pottery") Canyon, with 150 rooms stretching the length of a long shallow alcove, housed about 80 people; the other, Inscription House in a cave in Nitsin Canyon, contained about 80 rooms and housed around 75 people. Interpretive exhibits are provided at the visitor center, from which a half-mile trail leads to an overlook for viewing the canyon.

Access to the ruins is only with guided tours. Advance reservations are required for Keet Seel tours. To reach the monument from Tuba City, Arizona, drive northeast 50 miles on U.S. Route 160 and north nine miles on State Route 564. From Kayenta, Arizona, drive southwest 19 miles on Route 160 and north on Route 564.

Organ Pipe Cactus National Monument

Route 1, Box 100
Ajo, AZ 85321
520-387-6849
This 330,688-acre national monument adjacent to the U.S.-Mexican border in southwest Arizona protects an ecologically rich part of the Sonoran Desert. The area consists of jaggedly upthrusting mountains and an extraordinary variety of plants and animals that have adapted themselves in myriad fascinating ways to the intense heat and scant rainfall of this desert region. In addition to paloverde and desert ironwood trees and shrubs such as creosotebush and brittlebush, a multitude of such wildflowers as the goldpoppy, lupine, desert marigold, and owlclover burst into bloom and spread a carpet of color across the land in March and early April after winters of adequate rainfall. There are also 28 recorded species of cacti, including the tall saguaro and the many-stalked organpipe and senita. The great variety of wildlife includes the desert bighorn, javelina (peccary), coyote, rattlesnakes, Gila monster, phainopepla, pyrrhu-

loxia, roadrunner, Gambel quail, three kinds of doves, and the vermillion flycatcher.

Among several dirt roads in the monument, two loop through the desert: 21-mile Ajo Mountain Drive and 51-mile Puerto Blanco Drive. A highlight of the latter is the wildlife-rich oasis of pond and springs at Quitobaquito. The monument provides interpretive exhibits and programs at the visitor center, hiking trails, a campground, and picnic areas along the loop drives. Visitors are cautioned to avoid overexposure and overexertion.

Access to the monument's visitor center from I-8 at Gila Bend is south 74 miles on State Route 85 through Ajo and Why; or west 119 miles on State Route 86 from Tucson to Why and south 22 miles on State Route 85. The border crossing at Lukeville into Mexico is five miles south of the visitor center.

Pipe Spring National Monument

H.C. 65, Box 5
Fredonia, AZ 86022
520-643-7105
This 40-acre national monument north of the Grand Canyon in northern Arizona protects a ranch established in the early 1870s by Mormon pioneers. The "fort" consists of two, two-story stone houses facing each other across a courtyard and joined together with high walls—one of which contains a massive gate into the courtyard. While the fortification was built to afford protection against Indian raids, the ranch never came under attack. At the peak of the operation, more than 2,000 head of cattle were run on Pipe Spring Ranch.

At this memorial to the settlement of the region by early cattle ranchers and cowboys, visitors may see homes, bunk houses, work sheds, and corrals typical of 19th-century ranches. At certain seasons, visitors may also observe cattle being rounded up and herded into corrals and calves being branded. The visitor center provides interpretive exhibits and a short video, and a half-mile interpretive trail loops up an area of cliffs behind the historic structures. While there are no picnicking or camping facilities within the monument, the nearby Kaibab Paiute Indian Reservation offers options for both.

Access to the monument from Fredonia, Arizona, is west 14 miles on State Route 389. From St. George, Utah, drive north seven miles on I-15, east nine miles on Utah State Route 9 to Hurricane, Utah, and east 40 miles on Utah State Route 59 and Arizona State Route 389.

Rainbow Bridge National Monument

c/o Glen Canyon National
Recreation Area
P.O. Box 1507
Page, AZ 86040-1507
520-608-6404

Rainbow Bridge, the world's largest known natural sandstone arch, spans 275 feet and rises 290 feet above the bottom of Bridge Canyon in southeast Utah. The creation of the bridge began when the eroding power of flowing water broke through a section of the narrow pink sandstone wall in a sharp bend of the canyon's meandering stream. It was then gradually enlarged by rock falls and shaped by wind and rain. The Navajo Indians, whose reservation adjoins the 160-acre national monument, consider it a sacred place.

Until Glen Canyon Dam was completed on the Colorado River in 1963 and created Lake Powell, Rainbow Bridge was reached by a rugged 15-mile trek. While a few people still hike to the bridge (permits are required from the Navajo Nation), most visitors arrive by boat (boat tours are provided)—a 50-mile trip from Glen Canyon National Recreation Area's Wahweap, Halls Crossing, or Bullfrog marinas, and walk a short trail up from the boat dock to near the bridge.

Sunset Crater Volcano National Monument

6400 N. Highway 89
Flagstaff, AZ 86004
520-526-1157

Sunset Crater is a 1,070-foot-tall volcanic cinder cone with a 400-foot-deep crater at its summit, named for the reddish-colored cinders at its rim that glow at sunset. Located just east of the 12,643-foot San Francisco Peaks in northern Arizona, Sunset is the youngest of about 400 volcanoes in the million-acre San Francisco volcanic field. In the winter of A.D. 1064-65, molten rock suddenly and violently

exploded from within the earth, sending huge billowy clouds of ash, cinders, and volcanic bombs high into the sky. Periodic eruptions of cinders and ash continued over the next few decades, gradually creating the symmetrical black cone. The 3,040-acre national monument also protects lunar-like expanses of jagged, black lava flows that squeezed onto the land from under the base of the cinder cone.

While climbing Sunset Crater is not permitted to avoid damaging the unstable cinder slopes, an interpretive trail loops through part of the Bonita Lava Flow so that visitors may see a lava tube, spatter cones, squeeze-ups, and other features. Stately ponderosa pines are widely scattered across the flow and part way up the slopes of the cone. Interpretive exhibits are provided at a visitor center in the adjacent national forest, where a campground is also available. There is a small picnic area in the monument.

To reach the monument from Flagstaff, drive north about 12 miles on U.S. Route 89 and east two miles on the 35-mile Sunset Crater/Wupatki Road that runs through Sunset Crater and Wupatki national monuments and re-connects with Route 89. It is 15 miles from the Wupatki visitor center up to Sunset Crater.

Tonto National Monument

H.C. 02, Box 4602
Roosevelt, AZ 85545
520-467-2241

This 1,120-acre national monument protects the ruins of two cave-sheltered masonry pueblos overlooking Theodore Roosevelt Lake in central Arizona. From about A.D. 1150 to shortly after 1400, the native Salado people lived here and raised cotton, maize, beans, squash, and other crops along the nearby Salt River (Rio Salado), for which they were named. Today, a half-mile trail leads from the visitor center up to the 19-room lower ruins. Advance reservations are required to visit the 40-room upper ruins that are reached by a mile-and-a-half trail.

The monument provides interpretive exhibits and a picnic area, along with the opportunity to view a wide variety of Sonoran Desert flora, such as paloverde, ocotillo, and ten species of cacti, including the tall saguaro. The many species of wildlife include javelina (peccary), ringtail, Gambel quail, phainopepla, hooded and Scott's orioles, and three kinds of wrens.

To reach the monument from Apache Junction just east of Phoenix, drive east 53 miles on U.S. Route 60 and north 25 miles on State Route 88. Or drive northeast 50 miles on State Route 88, more than 20 miles of which is the narrow winding dirt road called the Apache Trail.

Tumacacori National Historical Park

P.O. Box 67
Tumacacori, AZ 85640
520-398-2341

Preserved here are the impressive remains of an early 19th-century Spanish Catholic mission church, San Jose de Tumacacori, that was built by the Franciscan order near the site first visited by Father Eusebio Francisco Kino in 1691. This priest was a member of the Jesuit order, which became the most powerful social and economic force in the region until its expulsion by the Spanish Crown in 1767. The mission influenced the O'odham, or Pima, Indian villagers of Tumacacori and was one of the northernmost outposts of the mission chain established by Franciscan priests in the late 1700s. The three-unit, 46-acre park also protects the eroded adobe ruins of a mid-18th-century Jesuit church and a visita (a church without a priest). Interpretive exhibits in the visitor center and ranger-led and self-guided tours of the Tumacacori church are available, as is a small picnic area.

Access to the park from Tucson is south 45 miles on I-19. From Nogales, Arizona, on the U.S.-Mexican border, drive north 19 miles on I-19.

Tuzigoot National Monument

P.O. Box 219
Camp Verde, AZ 86322
520-634-5564

Tuzigoot protects the masonry ruins of a Sinaguan Indian village, occupied between A.D. 1125 and 1400. Its name is an Apache word for "crooked water," in reference to a formerly sharp bend in the adjacent Verde River of central Arizona. The Sinagua (Spanish for "without water") were largely a farming people who planted crops of maize, beans, and squash and irrigated their fields with water from the river. The settlement was inhabited for a century by about 50 people living in a small cluster of rooms, but in the 1200s the population twice doubled as Sinaguan refugees moved here to escape severe drought conditions in outlying areas. At its peak of occupation, the pueblo contained more than 100 rooms built around the summit of a 120-foot-high ridge.

A visitor center provides interpretive exhibits and a self-guided interpretive path leads to the hilltop. Adjoining Tuzigoot is the ecologically significant Tavasci Marsh, habitat for numerous species of wildlife including the rare Yuma clapper rail. Many hope that this privately owned area may soon be added to the monument.

To reach the monument from the Cottonwood exit on I-17, drive northwest 12 miles on State Route 260 to Cottonwood, proceeding four-and-a-half miles on Route 260 (straight through town at stoplights, toward Clarkdale), and right onto the monument turnoff. From Sedona, drive south 18 miles on U.S. Route 89A to Cottonwood, then four-and-a-half miles on State Route 260 toward Clarkdale to the monument turnoff. From Prescott, drive north about six miles on U.S. Route 89, then north 31 miles on U.S. 89A (through the historic mining town of Jerome) and one-and-a-half miles through Clarkdale, and take a left onto the monument turn-off.

Wupatki National Monument

6400 N. Highway 89
Flagstaff, AZ 86004
520-526-1157

Impressive ruins of red sandstone pueblos are scattered across the high-desert landscape of this 35,422-acre national monument. Following the series of volcanic eruptions that began in A.D. 1064-65, creating nearby Sunset Crater cinder cone and spreading ash across a wide expanse, several southwestern Indian groups, notably the Sinagua and Anasazi, moved into this area. These people discovered that the thin layer of ash and cinders in the Wupatki Basin increased the retention of moisture in the soil beneath, thus enhancing the growing of crops. Throughout the 1100s, these people shared their skills in farming, pottery making, and the construction of stone masonry villages, which they inhabited until around A.D. 1225.

Major construction of this village occurred between A.D. 1120 and 1195. The Wupatki (a Hopi word meaning "tall house") contained up to 100 rooms, was four stories high, and housed about 125 men, women, and children. Adjacent to the pueblo are a circular dance plaza and a large oval masonry structure believed to have been a ballcourt, similar to those used by the Hohokam in southern Arizona and by the Aztecs and Mayans in Mexico.

Interpretive exhibits are provided at the visitor center, and a short path leads to the upper and lower Wupatki Ruins. Among other major ruins in the monument are Lomaki ("beautiful house"), reached by a short spur road and trail, and Wukoki ("big and wide house"), reached by a two-and-a-half-mile spur road near the visitor center. A picnic area is provided on a short spur road in the adjacent national forest. While camping is not permitted in the monument, a campground is located on the national forest just west of Sunset Crater National Monument.

To reach Wupatki from Flagstaff, drive north 27 miles on U.S. Route 89 and east into the monument on the Wupatki/Sunset Crater Road (the visitor center is about 13 miles east of the entrance). Alternatively, drive 12 miles north of Flagstaff on Route 89 and turn onto the Sunset Crater/Wupatki Road, which reaches the visitor center in about 21 miles.

NEW MEXICO

Aztec Ruins National Monument

P.O. Box 640
Aztec, NM 87410
505-334-6174

This 319-acre national monument protects the masonry ruins of a once-extensive Anasazi settlement in the Animas River Valley of northwest New Mexico. The main ruin consists of a three-story great house that contained at least 400 rooms and was built around an open ceremonial plaza. Within part of the plaza is a circu-

lar great kiva, carefully reconstructed in the 1930s, that was the central focus of the village's religious and ceremonial life. Misnamed after the Aztec Indians of Mesoamerica by early settlers, the pueblo was actually built and occupied in the 12th and early 13th centuries by the Anasazi, who were ancestors of today's Pueblo Indians.

Interpretive exhibits are provided at the visitor center. A small picnic area is available. Access to the monument is north of the city of Aztec, close to the junction of U.S. Route 550 (that runs between Farmington, New Mexico, and Durango, Colorado) and State Route 544.

Bandelier National Monument

H.C.R. 1, Box 1
Los Alamos, NM 87544
505-672-3861

Bandelier is a scenically and archaeologically outstanding 32,737-acre national monument, protecting part of the canyon-gashed Pajarito (Little Bird) Plateau on the southeastern flank of the Jemez Mountains of northern New Mexico. It was named in honor of ethnologist-historian Adolf F. Bandelier (1840-1914), who visited a number of the pueblo ruins of the Anasazi Indians in the area in the 1880s and studied the customs of their descendants, the Pueblo Indians who live along the northern Rio Grande.

The monument's entrance road descends into Frijoles Canyon, ending at the visitor center, where interpretive exhibits and programs are provided. From there, a path leads a quarter-mile up-canyon to the circular Tyuonyi Ruin. This 400-room masonry village, which was originally two and possibly three stories high, was occupied by about 100 men, women, and children from the late A.D. 1300s until perhaps the mid-1500s. It was built around an open central plaza containing three circular kivas that were the focus of the village's religious and ceremonial activities. On land around the village, the Indians raised crops of maize, beans, and squash. Extending 800 feet along the base of the nearby south-facing cliffs of the canyon is evidence of dwellings created by carving out rooms from the soft, compacted volcanic-ash rock, called tuff, and building three- or four-story masonry structures outward from the cliff base.

The Pajarito Plateau, into which Frijoles and other canyons have been eroded, resulted from two horrendously violent eruptions—1.4 and 1.2 million years ago—of adjacent Jemez Mountains volcanoes that sent billowing, silica-rich clouds of ash, gases, and cinders high into the sky. Much of this material fell back to earth around the flanks of the volcanoes, creating a surrounding plateau up to a thousand feet thick. These eruptions, among the largest in the history of the world, are believed to have been at least 600 times greater than the powerful 1980 eruption of Mount St. Helens in Washington state. The central core of the former volcanoes is today the beautiful and geologically significant Valles Caldera. Measuring over 15 miles across, the caldera consists of open, grassy expanses, such as Valle Grande, scattered pine-covered lava domes, and the surrounding forested rim.

A trail up the monument's Frijoles Canyon, along el Rito de los Frijoles (the Creek of the Beans), provides a delightful hike beneath narrowleaf cottonwoods, boxelders, ponderosa pines, Douglas firs, and clumps of Gambel's oaks. Down-canyon, this trail provides views of the upper and lower Frijoles Falls and descends into White Rock Canyon, where the once-free-flowing Rio Grande has been inundated since the late 1980s by the reservoir behind Cochiti Dam. Other trails wind throughout the monument's wilderness backcountry that includes Alamo and Capulin canyons. Wildlife includes elk at higher elevations, mule deer, tassel-eared Abert squirrels, and wild turkeys. A picnic area is available near the visitor center in Frijoles Canyon, and a campground is located on the plateau, near the monument entrance.

To reach the monument from Santa Fe, drive north 16 miles to Pojoaque, west 12 miles on State Route 502, and nine miles on State Route 4 to the entrance.

Capulin Volcano National Monument

P.O. Box 40
Capulin, NM 88414
505-278-2201
In this great volcanic area, lava erupted in three flows separated by long periods of inactivity between 8000 and 2350 B.C. The last series of eruptions created Capulin Volcano, whose conical form rises more than 1,000 feet above its base to 8,182 feet above sea level. The mountain consists chiefly of loose cinders, ash, and other rock debris, which were spewed out by successive eruptions and fell back upon the vent, piling up to form the conical mound. Among the vegetation on the cinder cone are low-growing Gambel oaks, a few clumps of quaking aspens, squawbush, and capulin (chokecherry).

Interpretive exhibits are provided at the visitor center for the 792-acre monument, and a picnic area is available. A two-mile road winds up the cinder cone; at the end of it is the mile-long Crater Rim Trail. Access to the monument from I-25 at Raton, New Mexico, is east 28 miles on U.S. Route 87 and from Capulin north three miles on State Route 325. From Clayton, New Mexico, drive west 44 miles on U.S. Route 87 and north three miles from Capulin.

Chaco Culture National Historical Park

P.O. Box 220
Nageezi, NM 87037
505-786-7014
Between A.D. 800 and 1130, Chaco Canyon in the vast high desert of northwest New Mexico became a major cultural center of the Anasazi Indians. These people raised crops of maize, beans, and squash along irrigated canyon bottomlands and built extensive multi-storied masonry pueblos that were connected with outlier villages by a 300-mile network of roadways.

This 33,974-acre park protects hundreds of archaeological sites, including 13 major Indian pueblo ruins that represent the highest point of prehistoric civilization in this region. The quality of masonry workmanship and monumental architecture and the complexity of social, economic, political, and ritual organization of community life at Chaco Canyon reached heights rarely if ever matched and never surpassed in the Four Corners region. The largest of the Chacoan greathouses is Pueblo Bonito, a D-shaped "apartment house" that stair-stepped up to four stories along the curved rear wall, contained about 800 rooms and 37 ceremonial kivas, and is believed to have housed more than a thousand men, women, and children at its peak.

Other nearby pueblo ruins include 500-room Chetro Ketl, which contained two great kivas, and 284-room Pueblo del Arroyo. From about A.D. 1075 and 1115, the peak population in all the Chaco Canyon pueblos is thought to have been between 5,000 and 6,000. However, a five-decade period of extended drought, beginning around A.D. 1130, led to the abandonment of Chaco Canyon and the settlements throughout the surrounding San Juan Basin.

The park's visitor center provides interpretive exhibits, interpretive walks through the ruins, and evening campfire programs are offered. A campground is located a mile from the visitor center. Access to the park from I-40 at Thoreau, New Mexico, is north 60 miles on State Routes 371 and 57; or from State Route 44 at either Blanco Trading Post or Nageezi southwest 26 miles on State Route 57. Caution: The unpaved stretches of Route 57 are occasionally made virtually impassable by wet conditions.

Continental Divide National Scenic Trail

U.S. Forest Service
P.O. Box 7669
Missoula, MT 59807
406-329-3150
This national scenic trail extends 3,200 miles from the Canadian to the Mexican border. So far, the longest designated stretch of this route extends nearly 800 miles from Glacier National Park in Montana to Yellowstone National Park in Wyoming. In addition to Glacier and Yellowstone, the trail runs through Rocky Mountain National Park in Colorado and several national forests. The trail runs adjacent to El Malpais National Monument in New Mexico.

El Malpais National Monument

P.O. Box 939
Grants, NM 87020
505-783-4774
El Malpais (Spanish for "the badlands") is a spectacular volcanic area created by numerous outpourings of lava and cinders, dating from 800,000 to less than 1,000 years ago. Among the varied volcanic features are large expanses of five lava flows, cinder cones including the

1,800-foot-tall Bandera Crater, spatter cones, ice caves, and a 17-mile-long lava tube system. The 114,276-acre national monument protects most of the core area under the National Park Service, while the surrounding 260,000-acre national conservation area is somewhat less protectively managed by the U.S. Bureau of Land Management.

At between 6,200 and 8,063 feet above sea level, El Malpais's jagged and twisted black lava-flow surfaces support a remarkably rich variety of vegetation. Among trees that grow slowly on this harsh environment—often producing fascinating asymmetrical shapes—are ponderosa and pinyon pines, juniper, quaking aspen, and Douglas fir. Paleoecology researchers there discovered a 900-year-old Douglas fir, the oldest known for this species. El Malpais is also rich in Anasazi and Pueblo Indian history, as archaeological research has shown that people have been living in and around this rugged area for 10,000 years. The peak of prehistoric occupancy was from A.D. 950 to 1350, when the Anasazi people of the Chacoan Culture established outlier villages in the vicinity of El Malpais. They visited places in the badlands of religious significance and hunted, gathered ice from caves, and foraged for plants containing herbal and medicinal properties. Today's nearby Zuni and Acoma Pueblo Indians trace their ancestry back to those earlier Anasazi.

An excellent panorama of El Malpais is from Sandstone Bluff Overlook, just off State Route 117, ten miles south of I-40. Continuing seven miles south along the eastern edge of the monument, visitors may see the spectacular sandstone arch, La Ventana, in the national conservation area. Several miles farther south, the road squeezes through the Narrows, between the edge of the lava flow and the base of the 400-foot sandstone bluffs. Eighteen miles south of I-40, a picnic area is available. The other main access to El Malpais is from I-40 at Grants southward 25 miles on State Route 53 to the Bandera Crater-Candeleria Ice Cave. As of this writing, this northwest corner of the monument is still privately owned, and a small fee is charged to walk the path to the cave or climb the cinder cone. An unpaved, high-clearance-vehicle road (County Route 42) skirts the west and south sides of El Malpais.

Caution: Hiking on the rugged lava rock is difficult and potentially hazardous, and it is easy to become disoriented and lost. Visitors are urged to be extremely careful.

El Morro National Monument

Route 2, Box 43
Ramah, NM 87321-9603
505-783-4226
A 200-foot-high sandstone mesa known as Inscription Rock or El Morro (Spanish for "headland") is the central focus of this 1,278-acre national monument in western New Mexico. The earliest inscriptions carved into the soft cliff are Anasazi petroglyphs portraying bighorn sheep and geometric designs. The earliest European inscription on the cliff face was written in 1605 by Juan de Onate, the Spanish explorer and colonist who established the first Hispanic settlement in what is now New Mexico. Numerous other Spaniards and then American explorers, U.S. military expeditions, emigrants, and railroad survey crews also left their names at El Morro. Atop the mesa are the ruins of two Indian pueblos that were occupied between A.D. 1275 and 1350. The larger of the two contained more than 800 rooms and housed at least 1,000 men, women, and children.

Interpretive exhibits and a video are presented at the visitor center. From there, a half-mile, self-guided interpretive trail loops by the base of El Morro. Another trail continues around the prow of the headland and climbs steeply up and over the top of the massive headland, passing by both pueblo ruins and offering a wonderful panorama. A picnic area is located near the visitor center, and a campground is adjacent to the entrance road.

To reach El Morro from I-40 at Grants, New Mexico, drive west 42 miles on State Route 53. From I-40 at Gallup, New Mexico, drive south 30 miles on State Route 602 and east 26 miles on State Route 53.

Fort Union National Monument

P.O. Box 127
Watrous, NM 87753
505-425-8025
Built in 1851, Fort Union ultimately became the largest military post and main supply depot for the Military Department of New Mexico, consisting of three forts constructed near the junction of the Mountain Branch and Cimarron Cutoff of the Santa Fe Trail. The national monument protects the ruins of this sprawling military installation that was the key supply and resting point at the western edge of the Great Plains. The largest visible network of Santa Fe Trail ruts can still be seen—remnants of the perilous 1,200-mile route across the vast Great Plains and into the Southwest. Fort Union soldiers were engaged in campaigns to stop raids and other hostilities by bands of Apaches, Comanches, Navajos, and Cheyennes, until peace was finally achieved in 1875.

A visitor center with interpretive exhibits and programs and a self-guided interpretive trail are provided in the 720-acre national monument. Living-history reenactments are also presented, and a picnic area is available. Access from I-25 is at the Fort Union National Monument-State Route 161 exit (two miles north of Watrous on I-25) and north eight miles on route 161.

Gila Cliff Dwellings National Monument

Route 11, Box 100
Silver City, NM 88061
505-536-9461
This 533-acre national monument consists of two units in southwest New Mexico. One unit protects the ruins of a village of the Mimbres Phase of the Mogollon Culture—one of about a hundred such pueblo sites built along the upper Mimbres and Gila rivers and occupied from about A.D. 1000 to 1200. The other unit features the Gila Cliff Dwellings. These adobe-and-stone structures, containing about 40 rooms in five deep caves overlooking Cliff Dweller Canyon, housed ten to 15 families of the Mogollon Culture beginning around A.D. 1290. The monument is surrounded by the Gila National Forest, in which is the nation's first designated wilderness area—the Gila Wilderness.

A visitor center provides interpretive exhibits, and there is a one-mile, self-guided interpretive loop trail to the cliff dwellings. Picnic sites and campgrounds are available in the adjacent national forest. Access to the monument from Silver City is north 44 miles on narrow, winding State Route 15.

Pecos National Historical Park

P.O. Drawer 418
Pecos, NM 87522-0418
505-757-6414

This 6,670-acre park protects the ruins of Pecos Pueblo, construction of which was begun around A.D. 1300. At its peak of occupation from the mid-1400s to the mid-1600s, the Indian village contained 700 rooms, rose to four and in some places five stories, and housed some 2,000 men, women, and children. It was strategically situated between the Great Plains and the Rio Grande Valley, at the southern end of the Sangre de Cristo Mountains of northern New Mexico, and was a major trading center with other Indian settlements. In 1540, a Spanish expedition led by Francisco Vasquez de Coronado visited this great village, then called Cicuye. In 1598, another group of Spaniards arrived in New Mexico to conquer the region for Spain and to convert the native peoples to Christianity.

The park protects the ruins of two Spanish colonial Catholic mission churches. The first, a massive adobe structure boasting six bell towers, was completed in 1621. When the Pueblo Indians of many villages rebelled against Spanish colonization in 1680, many Spaniards were killed and all others were forced to leave New Mexico; this church and those in other Indian villages were plundered and destroyed. But in 1692, Spanish forces returned, reconquered New Mexico, and built new churches. In 1705, a big new adobe church was begun at Pecos—the ruins of which are still visible today. The last few residents of Pecos Pueblo finally left in 1840, moving 60 miles west to live with the residents of Jemez Pueblo.

The park also contains sites relating to the Santa Fe Trail, the Union victory at the brief Battle of Glorieta Pass during the Civil War, and the historic Forked Lightning cattle ranch that includes more than two miles of ecologically significant riparian habitat along the Pecos River. The visitor center provides interpretive exhibits and a video; a 1.25-mile, self-guided interpretive path from the center leads through the pueblo and church ruins. A picnic area is also available.

Access to the park from Las Vegas, New Mexico, is from I-25 at the Rowe exit (#307) and north five miles on State Route 63. From Santa Fe, take I-25 to the Pecos-Glorieta exit (#299) and drive east about seven miles on State Route 50 to the town of Pecos, then south two miles on State Route 63.

Salinas Pueblo Missions National Monument

P.O. Box 496
Mountainair, NM 87036
505-847-2585

This three-unit, 1,071-acre national monument is located in the Estancia Basin of north-central New Mexico, between the Great Plains and the Rio Grande Valley. It protects the ruins of three major Pueblo Indian villages, at Gran Quivira, Abo, and Quarai, occupied from around A.D. 1300 to the 1670s, as well as the impressive ruins of associated 17th-century Spanish mission churches and conventos built by the Franciscan order of the Catholic Church to serve these pueblos. Under the direction of friars, the massive churches at Abo and Quarai were begun in the 1620s and constructed of masonry cut from the local red sandstone. At Gran Quivira, two consecutive churches were built of local whitish-gray limestone—a small church in the 1620s and a much larger, never-completed edifice in 1659. Of the three apartment-like pueblo complexes, Abo housed about 800 men, women, and children; Quarai about 600; and Gran Quivira (originally known as Las Humanas) 1,500 or more at the peak of occupation.

These Indians were essentially a farming people, growing crops of maize, beans, and squash and, prior to Spanish conquest of the region, carrying on active trading with other Pueblos to the northwest and with the nomadic Apache Indians. One of the products used in trade was salt, which they gathered from nearby playas or salt lagoons (salinas). After the conquest, Spanish demands placed upon the Pueblo people, the impact of frequent Apache raids, and a period of drought, famine, and epidemics of disease brought about the abandonment of these ancient villages. In the 1670s, the last few residents finally gave up and moved to pueblos along the Rio Grande.

The monument's visitor center, located one block west of the junction of U.S. Route 60 and State Route 55 in the town of Mountainair, provides interpretive exhibits and programs. Picnic areas are available at each unit, and campgrounds are provided in the nearby national forest and Manzano Mountain State Park. From Mountainair, to reach the Abo unit, drive west nine miles on U.S. 60 and a half-mile north on State Route 513. To reach the Quarai unit, drive north eight miles on State Route 55 and west one mile on the entrance road. To the Gran Quivira unit, drive south 26 miles on State Route 55.

Santa Fe National Historic Trail

Long Distance Trails Group Office
National Park Service
P.O. Box 728
Santa Fe, NM 87504-0728
505-988-6888
This national historic trail extends 1,200 miles from Old Franklin, Missouri; through Kansas, Oklahoma, and Colorado to Santa Fe, New Mexico. The route was initially a major 19th-century commercial and cultural link between the United States and Mexico.

There are currently 20 certified Santa Fe National Historic Trail sites and sections open to the public. The automobile highway tour route approximately following the trail is marked with the official trail logo. More than 50 federal, state, county, and municipal government agencies, private organizations, and private landowners are working cooperatively with the National Park Service on the trail project. Highlights along the trail include Pecos National Historical Park and Fort Union National Monument in New Mexico, Bent's Old Fort National Historic Site in Colorado, and Fort Larned National Historic Site in Kansas. Interpretive programs and exhibits include the Santa Fe Trail Center in Larned, Kansas; the National Frontier Trails Center in Independence, Missouri; the Santa Fe Trail Museum in Trinidad, Colorado; and the Morton County Historical Society Museum in Elkhart, Kansas.

White Sands National Monument

P.O. Box 1086
Holloman AFB, NM 88330-1086
505-479-6124
Near the northern end of the Chihuahuan Desert in the mountain-framed Tularosa Basin of southern New Mexico lies a great natural wonder: the world's largest expanse of gyp-sum sand dunes. The 143,732-acre national monument protects a major portion of these scenic waves of snowy-white, 30- to 50-foot dunes—best viewed in the contrasting light and shadow of early morning or late afternoon. What little desert vegetation grows on or adjacent to the White Sands includes soaptree yucca, Mormon tea, claretcup cactus, fourwing saltbush, and rabbitbrush. Coyotes, kit foxes, jackrabbits, kangaroo rats, roadrunners, and lizards are among the native wildlife.

The visitor center provides interpretive exhibits and refreshments, and there is a one-mile, self-guided interpretive trail in the dunes. Picnic areas are available at the end of the Dunes Drive. Caution: It is very easy to become disoriented and lost while walking across or between the dunes, so visitors are urged to be extremely careful. Access to the monument is directly off U.S. Routes 70/82, 15 miles southwest of Alamogordo or 54 miles northeast of Las Cruces.

OKLAHOMA

Chickasaw National Recreation Area

P.O. Box 201
Sulphur, OK 73086
405-622-3165
This 9,988-acre national recreation area is named to honor the Chickasaw Indians, the original occupants of this land. In 1855, this area became part of the Chickasaw Nation, and a small part of the Indian lands was subsequently sold to the U.S. government for a public reservation.

The partly wooded, partly prairie-covered, gently rolling hills of south-central Oklahoma and its lakes, springs, and streams offer opportunities for boating, swimming, hiking on 18 miles of trails, and other outdoor recreational activities. In addition, bromide, sulphur, and other springs there have long been believed to have healing powers. Perhaps 7,000 years ago, native peoples sought out the healing properties of these springs, and more recently, Choctaws, Comanches, Caddos, and other Indians came for the waters.

Interpretive exhibits and programs are provided at the Travertine Nature Center, and there are interpreter-guided nature walks offering possible glimpses of a wide variety of wildlife, including whitetail deer, coyotes, foxes, opossums, armadillos, wild turkeys, bobwhite quail, roadrunners, and scissor-tailed flycatchers. Picnic areas and a campground are also available.

The Travertine District, in which are located many historic springs, Travertine and Rock creeks, and most of the hiking trails, is adjacent to the city of Sulphur and is accessed south from the city on U.S. Route 177. Lake of the Arbuckles reservoir is reached from several directions, including south of the Travertine District on U.S. Route 177 and west on either Cedar Blue or Buckhorn road; or just west of the city of Sulphur on State Route 7 and south on Point Road.

Oklahoma City National Memorial

P.O. Box 323
Oklahoma City, OK 73101
405-235-3313
This national memorial sits on three acres of land and commemorates the tragic and sudden loss of American lives in the bombing of the Alfred P. Murrah federal building April 19, 1995. The memorial was established in honor of the 168 victims and their families. The memorial offers the chance for peaceful contemplation and reflection: 168 empty stone chairs—one for every life lost—sit in the footprint of the Murrah building at the base of a terraced green lawn, guarded by a stand of evergreens. The chairs face a rectangular reflecting pool and a lone American elm that survived the bomb's blast, a symbol of hope for survivors and their loved ones. President Clinton authorized $5 million in federal money for construction and maintenance of the memorial and groundbreaking for the memorial's construction occurred in October 1998.

Until the memorial is completed, visitors may take a virtual tour of the Oklahoma City Memorial at www.Oklahoman.net/connections/memorial. For more information, contact the Oklahoma City National Memorial Foundation at 405-235-3313.

Trail of Tears National Historic Trail

Long Distance Trails Group Office
National Park Service
P.O. Box 728
Santa Fe, NM 87504-0728
505-988-6888
This trail marks two of the routes that were used from June 1838 to March 1839 in the forced removal of more than 16,000 Cherokee Indians from their ancestral lands in Georgia, Alabama, North Carolina, and Tennessee. Thousands of Cherokee people perished along the way. The first major relocation route extended 1,226 miles by water from Chattanooga, Tennessee; down the Tennessee, Ohio, and Mississippi rivers to the Arkansas River and ended near Tahlequah, Oklahoma, a community that today serves as the Cherokee Nation's headquarters. The second relocation route extended 826 miles by land, from Chattanooga through Nashville, Tennessee, and Hopkinsville, Kentucky; crossed the Mississippi River at Cape Girardeau, Illinois, continued through Rolla and Springfield, Missouri, and ended at Tahlequah.

Interpretive programs and exhibits are presented at such places as the Cherokee National Museum in Tahlequah, the Museum of the Cherokee Indian, in Cherokee, North Carolina, and the Trail of Tears State Park, in Missouri. Automobile tour routes, from Charleston, Tennessee, to Tahlequah are marked with signs containing the official trail logo. The national historic trail is the cooperative project involving the National Park Service, other federal, state, and local governmental agencies, the Cherokee Nation, the Eastern Board of Cherokee Indians, private landowners, and private organizations, such as the Trail of Tears Association, 1100 N. University, Suite 133, Little Rock, AR 72207; 501-666-9032.

Washita Battlefield National Historic Site

P.O. Box 890
Cheyenne, OK 73628
580-497-2742
This 330-acre national historic site commemorates the attack on November 27, 1868, of a Cheyenne Indian village. Under the command

of Lt. Col. George A. Custer the 7th U.S. Cavalry killed 50 to 60 Cheyenne men, women, and children, including Chief Black Kettle. The site consists of a mixed-grassland prairie habitat and some cottonwoods that border the river.

Visitors are advised to stop first at the state-run Black Kettle Museum in Cheyenne, where a trail guide to the Washita Battlefield site is available. The Upper Trail leads .8-mile through Custer's command area, the pony-kill site, and the place where Major Joel Elliot, the second-in-command, was last seen. The Lower Trail winds .7-mile through the site believed to have been occupied by the Cheyenne village and along the banks of the Washita River and affords a view of the area from which Custer launched his attack. Interpretive programs are provided seasonally. A picnic area is available. Access to the site from I-40 at Sayre is north 25 miles on U.S. Route 283 to the Black Kettle Museum. From there, the national historic site is west two miles on State Route 47A. The museum is open daily in the summer and on Tuesdays through Sundays the rest of the year.

TEXAS

Alibates Flint Quarries National Monument

c/o Lake Meredith National Recreation Area
P.O. Box 1460
Fritch, TX 79036
806-857-3151
For at least 12,000 years, native peoples quarried, flaked, and formed arrowheads, spear points, knives, drills, and other tools from the agatized dolomite at the quarries now protected within this 1,370-acre national monument in the Texas panhandle. Some of the earliest users of these flint quarries were of the Clovis, Folsom, and other early cultures dating from around 10,000 to 6,000 years ago; they made spears for hunting mammoths, bison, and other game. Much more recently, farming peoples crafted tools and items for trade.

Interpretive exhibits are provided at the Bates Canyon Information Center, in Lake Meredith National Recreation Area. Ranger-led interpretive tours are offered during the summer and by reservation the rest of the year. A one-mile interpretive trail is available. There are picnic areas and campgrounds in the adjacent Lake Meredith National Recreation Area. To reach the monument from Amarillo, drive north about 30 miles on State Route 136 and five miles on Alibates Road to the information center. From Fritch, drive south six miles on State Route 136 and five miles on Alibates Road.

Amistad National Recreation Area

H.C.R. 3, Box 5J
Del Rio, TX 78840-9350
830-775-7491
Amistad (Spanish for "friendship") is a 58,500-acre national recreation area, stretching along the U.S.-Mexican border in southwest Texas. Amistad Reservoir, created behind six-mile-long Amistad Dam, extends 74 miles up the Rio Grande, 14 miles up the Pecos River, and 25 miles up the Devils River. The reservoir offers a wide variety of water-based activities, including boating, water-skiing, swimming, and scuba diving. The national recreation area also protects some of the world's most spectacular prehistoric rock art, including murals more than 100 feet long and 9,000 years old.

The information center, just west of Del Rio on U.S. Route 90, provides interpretation and orientation, and there are ranger stations at various locations. Picnic areas, campgrounds, interpretive trails, and boat ramps are available. Access to the national recreation area headquarters is just west of Del Rio on U.S. Route 90. The closest routes from there to the lake are about six miles.

Big Thicket National Preserve

3785 Milam
Beaumont, TX 77701
409-839-2689
Known as a "biological crossroads" of North America, 96,679-acre Big Thicket in southeast Texas was established to protect an extraordinary variety of species that coexist in this rainy, humid, and ecologically complex area. The national preserve is comprised of eight land units and four water-corridor units. Habitats

include cypress swamps and bayous, virgin pine and hardwood forests, plains and sandhills, and even a touch of southwestern desert. More than 85 species of trees, 60 flowering shrubs, and 5,000 flowering plants have been identified. Among the trees are bald cypress, four varieties of pine, southern magnolia, American sycamore, seven kinds of hickories, eleven species of oaks, and flowering dogwood. Shrubs include azalea and dwarf palmetto. Among the more than 300 species of resident and migratory birds are the anhinga, herons, egrets, a long list of migratory warblers, the colorful painted bunting, and the roadrunner that is typical of the Desert Southwest. Mammals include armadillos, whitetail deer, foxes, and opossums. In addition, 50 species of reptiles have been identified, including such poisonous snakes as water moccasins, rattlesnakes, copperheads, and coral snakes.

The preserve's visitor information center is located at the south end of the Turkey Creek Unit, seven miles north of Kountze, Texas, on U.S. Route 69 and east 2.5 miles on FM Route 420. Interpretive programs offered there include interpreter-led walks, boat tours, and canoe trips (for reservations and information, call 409-246-2337). There are numerous hiking trails in the preserve, including several self-guided interpretive trails. Picnic areas are provided. Backcountry camping is allowed with a free permit in some of the units, and campgrounds are available on nearby lands. Boating is popular on a number of the preserve's waterways, including the Neches River. Caution: Visitors should be alert for poisonous snakes, fire ants, chiggers, ticks, poison ivy, and cat brier vines.

Chamizal National Memorial

800 S. San Marcial Street
El Paso, TX 79905
915-532-7273
Chamizal, along the Rio Grande in El Paso, Texas, is a 55-acre memorial to international cooperation and good will achieved through peaceful diplomacy and marks specifically the peaceful end to a 99-year boundary dispute between the United States and Mexico. The Chamizal Treaty of 1963 ended a long-festering disagreement over a controversial tract of land created when the Rio Grande changed its course. The final agreement launched a plan to build a concrete-lined channel for the Rio Grande, following the mutually agreed-upon compromise boundary, and inspired the memorial honoring the cultural heritages of both nations. The memorial presents historical and art exhibits and a documentary video and sponsors cultural programs of the performing and visual arts. A picnic area is available. Access from I-10 is onto either Paisano Drive or Delta Street to S. San Marcial Street to the entrance. Across the river channel, Mexico has established its own park and an outstanding archaeological museum.

Fort Davis National Historic Site

P.O. Box 1456
Fort Davis, TX 79734
915-426-3224
This 460-acre national historic site adjacent to the scenic Davis Mountains of west Texas protects the best-preserved historic U.S. military fort in the Southwest. From 1854 to 1891, its troops provided protective military escorts for freight wagons and stagecoaches on the San Antonio-to-El Paso road, as Apache Indians fought to retain control of this region.

The remnants of this key fort are today more extensive and impressive than those of any other fort in the Southwest. Twenty percent of the original buildings have been restored. The visitor center provides interpretive exhibits and a video, and there is a self-guided walk through the grounds and several of the authentically refurnished structures. Living-history demonstrations and guided tours are presented during the summer. A picnic area is available, and there is a campground at nearby Davis Mountains State Park. Access is from I-10 at Balmorhea and south on State Route 17; from I-10 at Kent and south on State Route 118; from U.S. Route 90 at Alpine, driving north 24 miles on State Route 17; or from U.S. Route 90 at Marfa, driving north about 21 miles on State Route 118.

Lake Meredith National Recreation Area

P.O. Box 1460
Fritch, TX 79036
806-857-3151
Lake Meredith, on the Canadian River in the Texas panhandle, is a popular 44,977-acre national recreation area. This reservoir behind

Sanford Dam contrasts spectacularly with surrounding rock walls, pinnacles, and buttes. Boating, sailing, water skiing, swimming, and scuba diving are popular. A marina, boat-launching ramps, picnic areas, and campgrounds are available. Bates Canyon information center serves both the recreation area and adjacent Alibates Flint Quarries National Monument. Access is north on State Route 136 from Amarillo or south from Fritch, and then west five miles on Alibates Road.

Lyndon B. Johnson National Historical Park

P.O. Box 329
Johnson City, TX 78636
830-868-7128

This 1,570-acre park in the central Texas hill country includes the birthplace, boyhood home, and ranch of Lyndon B. Johnson, the 36th president of the United States (1963-69), along with his grandparents' log cabin and the Johnson family cemetery. The site commemorates President Johnson's 40-year record of achievements as a teacher, public official, and elder statesman.

The main visitor center, located near the entrance of Lyndon B. Johnson State Park, offers interpretive exhibits and programs. Bus tours (fee charged) of the national historical park begin there. In Johnson City, the park's center is located at 100 Lady Bird Lane, near the LBJ boyhood home, where guided tours are offered. Access to both parts of the national historical park are on U.S. Route 290: Johnson City is 50 miles west of Austin; and the LBJ Ranch unit and state park are about 64 miles west of Austin or 16 miles east of Fredericksburg.

Padre Island National Seashore

9405 South Padre Island Drive
Corpus Christi, TX 78418-5597
512-949-8173

This 130,434-acre national seashore on the Texas gulf coast protects 68 miles of barrier island beaches, along with sand dunes, scattered marshy swales, grassland plains, and tidal flats—one of the longest stretches of primitive, undeveloped ocean beach in the United States. Many of the dunes are stabilized with grasses, such as dropseed and sea oats. Two

species of yuccas, sweetbay, mesquite, a few live oak trees, and many kinds of wildflowers grow on North and South Padre islands. Whitetail deer, coyotes, and badgers are among the seashore's mammals; while white pelicans, white ibises, spoonbills, and sandhill cranes are among the more than 400 bird species. Five species of endangered sea turtles are also found there.

Interpretive exhibits are presented at the Malaquite Beach visitor center, and interpretive programs and a self-guided trail are provided. A campground and concession store are located at Malaquite Beach. Open camping is permitted on certain stretches of the seashore. For a recorded message on beach conditions, call 512-949-8175. Access from Corpus Christi is over the causeway to North Padre Island on State Route 358, and south on Park Road 22.

Palo Alto Battlefield National Historic Site

1623 Central Blvd. , #213
Brownsville, TX 78520
956-541-2785

This 391-acre national historic site, just north of Brownsville, Texas, commemorates the first territorial dispute of the Mexican-American War of 1846-1848. The Battle of Palo Alto on the plains near the Rio Grande on May 8, 1846, ended with the withdrawal of the Mexican troops across the river. Even though U.S. soldiers were substantially outnumbered (2,300 Americans to 3,200 Mexicans) American weapons were far superior and caused far greater casualties.

Limited visitor facilities include interpretive exhibits, a video, and publications at the national historic site's office in Brownsville. Interpretive kiosks and wayside panels can be found at the parking area and along a short path at the site, just off Farm Route 1847. NPCA has been supporting the proposal to expand this site to 3,400 acres to more adequately protect and interpret this important historical event. The site's office is open on weekdays, except on federal holidays.

Rio Grande Wild and Scenic River

c/o Big Bend National Park
P.O. Box 129
Big Bend National Park, TX 79834
915-477-2251

Beginning in Big Bend National Park with Marascal and Boquillas canyons and continuing downstream to the Terrell Val Verde county line, this protected riverway is a 191-mile-long strip along the U.S. bank of the Rio Grande, which forms west Texas's border with Mexico. This remote, undeveloped Chihuahuan Desert area is popular for rafting and canoeing, for which a float permit is required. There are no federal facilities downstream from Big Bend National Park and no take-out points for 83 miles. (See text on Big Bend National Park for further information on rafting and canoeing the Rio Grande.)

San Antonio Missions National Historical Park

2202 Roosevelt Avenue
San Antonio, TX 78210-4919
210-534-8833
This 819-acre park protects four Spanish frontier mission churches established in the 18th century along the San Antonio River in south-central Texas. The missions were primarily religious centers and training grounds for Spanish citizenship. They offered the Coahuiltecan Indians of this area an easier transition into European culture by concentrating scattered tribes into self-sufficient, church-oriented communities. The missions are still active Catholic parishes today.

The visitor center, located in the Mission San Jose unit, provides historical exhibits and videos. Interpretive talks and tours are also available at the four units. In the Mission San Juan unit, a short interpretive nature trail winds along the river. Facilities for picnicking and camping are located near the park. Access to Mission San Jose and the park's visitor center from I-37 is at the W. Southcross exit, then west on Southcross and left onto Roosevelt Avenue to the park. Directions to the other park units may be obtained at the visitor center or by telephoning the park.

Friends of the Parks Organizations

Big Thicket Association
P.O. Box 198
Saratoga, TX 77585
409-262-8522

Big Thicket Conservation Association
9713 Mariposa
Houston, TX 77025
713-667-7809

Chickasaw NRA Park Support Committee
113 W. Muskogee
Sulphur, OK 73086
405-622-2824

Continental Divide Trail Society
3704 N. Charles Street, Suite 601
Baltimore, MD 21218
410-235-9610

Friends of Bandelier
P.O. Box 1282
Los Alamos, NM 87544
505-665-7769

Friends of Capulin Volcano
P.O. Box 40
Capulin, NM 88414
505-278-2201

Friends of Ft. Davis
P.O. Box 944
Ft. Davis, TX 79734
915-426-3844

Friends of Lake Powell
P.O. Box 7007
Page, AZ 86040
520-645-1853

Friends of Saguaro National Park
P.O. Box 18998
Tucson, AZ 85731-9998
520-298-3258

Friends of the Albuquerque Petroglyphs
2920 Carlyle, NE
Albuquerque, NM 87110
505-889-3779

Friends of Walnut Canyon
330 S. Ash
Flagstaff, AZ 86004
520- 526-4804

Grand Canyon Association
P.O. Box 399
Grand Canyon, AZ 86023
520-638-2481

Grand Canyon River Guides
P.O. Box 1934
Flagstaff, AZ 86002
520-773-1075

Grand Canyon Trust
2601 N. Fort Valley Road
Flagstaff, AZ 86001
520-774-7488

Los Amigos del Malpais
P.O. Box 2336
Milan, NM 87021
505-285-6173

Los Amigos de Tumacacori
P.O. Box 67
Tumacacori, AZ 85640
520-398-2341

Los Compadres de San Antonio Missions
6701 San Jose Drive
San Antonio, TX 78214
210-922-3218

Santa Fe Trail Association
Santa Fe Trail Center
Route 3
Larned, KS 67550
316-285-2054

Save the Jemez
515 Tulane Place, NE
Albuquerque, NM 87110
505-266-2002

Trail of Tears Association
1100 N. University, Suite 133
Little Rock, AR 72207
501-666-9032

Cooperating Associations

Archaeological Conservancy, The
5301 Central Avenue, NE, Suite 1218
Albuquerque, NM 87108
505-266-1540

Big Bend Natural History Association
P.O. Box 68
Big Bend National Park, TX 79834
915-477-2236

Carlsbad Caverns-Guadalupe Mountains
Natural History Association
P.O. Box 1417
Carlsbad, NM 88221
505-785-2365

Glen Canyon Natural History Association
P.O. Box 581
Page, AZ 86040
520-645-3532

Grand Canyon Natural History Association
P.O. Box 399
Grand Canyon, AZ 86023
520-638-2481

National Trust for Historic Preservation
1785 Massachusetts Avenue, NW
Washington, DC 20036
202-673-4000

Petrified Forest Museum Association
P.O. Box 2277
Petrified Forest Nat'l Park, AZ 86028
520-524-6224

Southwest Parks and Monuments Association
211 N. Court Avenue
Tucson, AZ 85701
520-622-1999

Student Conservation Association
1800 N. Kent Street
Arlington, VA 22209
703-524-2441

L O C A L   C O L O R

The Wildlife

"Texas" means friend.

Texas was a country before it was a state.

25 languages.

65 nationalities.

Texans believe life is too important to be dull.

The Wildflowers

The state flower is the Bluebonnet.

Over 5,000 species of wildflowers.

There's even a Wildflower Center (Thanks to Lady Bird Johnson).

Texas does not have blue grass. It just seems that way.

It's like a whole other country.

Even the vacations are bigger in Texas. From the yarn-spinning charm of our native citizenry to hills carpeted with our native flowers, you'll find it all in Texas. It's more than you think. It's like a whole other country. For your free Texas travel guide, you can visit our web site at 💻 **www.TravelTex.com** or call us at ☎ **1-800-8888-TEX (Ext. 1290).** So give us a call, y'all.